After Law

After Law

Laurent de Sutter

Translated by Barnaby Norman

polity

Originally published in French as *Après la loi* © Presses Universitaires de France/Humensis, *Après la loi*, 2018

This English edition © Polity Press, 2021

This work received the French Voices Award for excellence in publication and translation. French Voices is a program created and funded by the French Embassy in the United States and FACE Foundation (French American Cultural Exchange). French Voices Logo designed by Serge Bloch.

Polity Press
65 Bridge Street
Cambridge CB2 1UR, UK

Polity Press
101 Station Landing
Suite 300
Medford, MA 02155, USA

ISBN-13: 978-1-5095-4236-9
ISBN-13: 978-1-5095-4237-6 (pb)

A catalogue record for this book is available from the British Library.

Library of Congress Cataloging-in-Publication Data

Names: De Sutter, Laurent, author. | Norman, Barnaby, translator.
Title: After law / Laurent de Sutter ; translated by Barnaby Norman.
Other titles: Après la loi. English
Description: Cambridge, UK ; Medford, MA : Polity Press, [2020] | Includes bibliographical references and index. | Summary: "Why law may be less important than we think"-- Provided by publisher.
Identifiers: LCCN 2020020737 (print) | LCCN 2020020738 (ebook) | ISBN 9781509542369 (hardback) | ISBN 9781509542376 (paperback) | ISBN 9781509542383 (epub) | ISBN 9781509545438 (adobe pdf)
Subjects: LCSH: Law--Philosophy. | Law (Philosophical concept) | Law--History.
Classification: LCC K230.D4343 D4713 2020 (print) | LCC K230.D4343 (ebook) | DDC 340/.1--dc23
LC record available at https://lccn.loc.gov/2020020737
LC ebook record available at https://lccn.loc.gov/2020020738

Typeset in 10.5 on 12pt Sabon
by Fakenham Prepress Solutions, Fakenham, Norfolk NR21 8NL
Printed and bound in Great Britain by TJ Books Limited

For further information on Polity, visit our website:
politybooks.com

For Serge Gutwirth

Contents

Translator's Note

The English translation of *Après la loi* – *After Law* –
presents a particular problem, apparent in the final word
of the title and traversing the entire text until the last
sentence of the Postlude. Put simply, the English language
collapses two concepts that are separated in the French
terms 'loi' and 'droit' into the single all-embracing 'law'.
In some ways, this is a striking confirmation of one of the
central theses of the work: that over the course of Western
history, the law, 'la loi', with everything it entails in terms
of abstraction and normativity, has come to dominate
and determine the concrete and casuistic 'droit'. The
obvious solution, and the one used throughout this work
is to translate 'loi' with 'law' and 'droit' with 'right'. This
procedure is not, however, perfect, and carries certain
risks. The most significant of these is that 'right' in English
has come to be associated almost exclusively with the
'rights' of the 'subject', which is to say the individual rights
the subject embodies within a political construct. 'Right',
as it is predominantly used in this work, is better understood in its opposition to 'Law': a disruptive activity of
becoming that challenges, perhaps deconstructs, the *being*
of Law. All this becomes most explicit in the 'Postlude',
which returns to all the oppositions in play throughout the
work as it passes through a global series of legal traditions.
Throughout the English text, as it builds to this finale,
I have, therefore, capitalized 'Law' and 'Right' when

they are clearly to be understood in the tension of this opposition. This is intended to serve as a visual reminder that neither 'Law' nor 'Right' quite map onto the common meanings the terms carry in English, and it will be to some degree the responsibility and the experience of the reader to come to an understanding of how they operate across this text.

Foreword

Avital Ronell

Our relation to the law is not easy to untangle or tame using merely historical narrative. Fortunately, Laurent de Sutter provides us with a scanning apparatus, hermeneutically fine-tuned, by which to measure essential prompts of juridical life. With the care of a relentlessly searching analysis, his text hands us a number of flagged contracts to renegotiate and, where necessary, to repudiate.

We know that, beginning with Cleisthenes' fateful intervention, philosophers bristled while they defended the *demos*, worried about the takeover of a mob primed to go off locked and loaded, lawless and intemperate. *After Law* offers a sweeping historical account of conceptual overhauls that are responsible for boosting democratic tenacity in the face of so many obstacles and their punctual power failures. Perhaps now more than ever our legal and juridical inheritance presses upon us, urging a review of a speculative jurisprudence that involves an untold history and stealth attack plans.

Timely and incisive, this work repurposes our juridical scaffolding, making allowances for wide-ranging effects of existential fallout in the political realms that affect us today. It faces down the transcendental assumptions that fuel our relation to the law and its legally constellated satellites. Without explicitly calling up psychoanalytic theory, *After Law* locates the power-pump of social narcissism and forms of *drivenness* that undergird an abiding relation to the law. We are given to understand that, like Kafka's man from the country, one's condition of sheer stuckness 'before the law' cannot be abrogated. This predicament holds for a diverse and often incompatible cultural rhetoric of law and governance, a temporal span that involves the subtle implications of finding oneself called *before* the law only to be snagged *after* the law's epoch of authority.

On civic alert, Professor de Sutter examines the moves that were made historically in order to supplant familial logic with the idea of Law and the implementation of human rights. He trains his analysis on distinctions drawn by the fundamental juridical structures reconfigured under structural mutation, their emergence and inherent instabilities – in some cases, their unapologetic takeover stratagems. The text's questioning looks at the foundational yet elusive facets of law and aporias of power. Its microanalyses interrogate the workings of Law, constitutions, penal codes, institutions, acts of positing and the co-implicating force of hypothetical judgement that hold them together as well as apart. The account of juridical presuppositions reflects the processes of corresponding historical changes in political vocabularies. So that 'no tyranny could ever return', the reigning god or legislator in Greek legal arbitration had to be replaced by the City itself, a repartition involving a new understanding of *sharing* together with an ever new distribution of civic responsibility. The strife between human *nomos* and divine *nomos*, in the limited yet self-replicating instance of ancient Greek philosophy, has had to be renegotiated at crucial junctures in modernity. At one point, the agonistic terms of law-giving powers reappear with the *Spaltung* (split-off) discussed in Walter Benjamin's reflections on law and violence in terms of the striking force that differentiates human from divine law. Yet, how do we live with a relation to law whose authority is eroding?

In Freudian terms of social pessimism, it may well be the case that we will never be able to effect a jailbreak from narcissistic lockdown and expunge the vacuity of shameless self-promotion that pervades our times, exercising a reckless disregard for the rule of law and its principled apportionment of equality. We're neither the only nor the first ones to contend with encroaching morphs in despotism, the chokehold of a lawless political organization. De Sutter's argument indicates that every social body on record has been tempted by tyrannical excess.

Ensnarled in familialisms and archaic structures of troubled coexistence, each phase of civilization has registered a will to break free of local bullying tendencies, hoping to dissolve tenacious political strangleholds. The tyrannical impulse exposed by Plato's legendary analyses and the refinements of Aristotle's political warning system exemplifies philosophical pushback on autocratic incursions. In the assertive span of Athenian juridical life, Cleisthenes was the first to call up Greek democracy. Not everyone in the history of philosophy was on board with the initial rallying call, and certainly no philosopher proved more ready to march along with a destructive politics than Martin Heidegger in 1934. What does this tell us about philosophers –not to say of formations of will-to-power, and the enduring appeal, whether heeded or dismissively cast, made in theoretical studies of Law?

By now, we know this much: the tyrant, whether on the loose or held in place, is always ready to pounce, breaking out of a republic of unchecked phantasms and into states of lawless abandon. According to the tag-team of Plato and Freud, one falls into tyranny when betraying the democratic model of paternal legacy, squeezing out the law internalized, honoured, remembered. Superego and the *inheritance* it implies are kicked to the curb, fully divested by the tyrant who, according to Plato, has snuffed out paternal mimesis and regulatory hand-downs.

The law and its representatives are disseminated by various institutions and positing acts that exercise a provisional flex of power. Where regulatory habits are disdained, if arbitrarily applied, and surveillance mechanisms idle on the edge of lawful intrusion have spread with viral tenacity, we need to contend with crucial questions of a primary order. Why are we governed by laws, and who gets to escape their alternatively crude and sophisticated forms of punishing inscription? How do we account for the historicity and cultural codifications of Law that reassert its authority – or expose transcendental principles as problematic and wobbly? And, to introduce a perspective covered in Derrida's reflections on Benjamin's essay 'The Critique of Violence', what is the force of Law? How does it determine or overdetermine culpability, axioms of retribution and various forms of juridical sentencing? Is the regime of legal violence inescapable once a subject is placed in signifying chains?

Jean-François Lyotard, for his part, takes up the juridical shortfall in *The Differend*, a theoretical rollout citing the need for a pushback on legal falsification, gestures that could not be registered by techniques of legal review: a nervous tic, a blush, a hysterical cough, yet another somatic outbreak such as hives, or the resolute silence of a torture victim. Lyotard folded these unlitigatable shudders into what he named a 'phrasal regimen'. The phrasal regimen covers an entire syntax of extra-legal efforts to speak a truth before a court without reverting to a strictly coded and pre-authorized rhetoric. These efforts involve releasing new types of information on the semiotic build-up of a distressed body under interrogation, its attendant symptomatologies, including the inability to say what one has witnessed or recount the violence to which one has been made to succumb. In *Masochism: Coldness and Cruelty*, Gilles Deleuze outlines the masochist's presuppositions of lawful adherence, whereas Jacques Lacan, in 'Kant with Sade', brings up the rear with his anal-sadistic location shot for the juridical disposition. There's more to this line-up because the cartography of the legal impingement on our lives – intimate, body-bound and insidious – is as complicated as it is prevalent. In the wake of Kafka's grammar of hypothetical speculation, it has become impossible, argues Lyotard, to prove one's innocence. Kafka was already driving while Black, steering a minority's literature of legal despair.

In these times, what still passes for 'human relations' seems irremediably beholden to legal institutions and conceptual grids. The prediction made by de Tocqueville about the modern democratic state rings true: the citizenry will have complied with the *juridification* of all relations. No moment of interiority will be spared legal assignment, interrogation or potential dispute. (I amp up for effect. Alexis de Tocqueville had enough problems on his hands without having to trifle with a presumed subject's 'interiority' and other Hegelian acrobatics.) Tyrannical breakouts have separated off from paternal law – and, we could add, calling upon a pending Kleinian politics, that the tyrannically seized soul has failed to internalize the good breast, to learn repair or submit to reparative justice. Is the commitment to reparative justice still something we can imagine, if only as a regulatory ideal, an aneconomic gift? It seems as though we must do so, imagine and commit to repair, even if Heinrich von Kleist has made the aporias of repair undefeatable for us moderns.

PRELUDE

§*A. Law.* For more than two thousand years, the West has lived under the rule of Law – a jealous rule, which tolerates infractions only insofar as they are the means by which offenders come to recognize anew its incontestable supremacy. This dominion was not built in a day, and has not failed to provoke resistance; but the *legal proposition* possessed, it would seem, a persuasiveness that its rivals did not: it won. Looking carefully at its contemporary form, it is possible to understand why: behind Law, there extends a whole domain of thought, valorizing order, reason, coherence, power and security. Even today, this domain of thought constitutes the default regime for everything, from university research to café conversation – from the perspective of this regime, anything escaping the parameters of the domain in question would lead to chaos. And the fear of chaos is without doubt the dominant psychological factor in the ecology of Law: the fear that something should flee, dodge, escape the lawful state of things, and in this way, reveal it to be nothing. *The real is what Law fears*: the whole history of the progressive triumph of the idea of Law in the West can be reread in light of this maxim, which might be thought of as embodying, in an originary way, its inexpressible. By this, we must understand that what Law fears most is not the real as such, but *its* own real, everything that traverses it and makes it possible – but that makes it possible only by being excluded from its discourse. Excluding its own real is, moreover, the most essential task to which the category of Law has been devoted since the beginning: Law is what works to exclude its own real – Law is what accomplishes its own closure on its blind spot. This beginning is Greek and philosophical, where the real that the category of Law sought to exclude was that of Right, as though Law only existed to make Right impossible except under its exclusive direction.[1] In this way, the most precious juridical treasures were forgotten, and with them countless inventions allowing for the imagination of unregulated lives and societies that would yearn for movement. After Law, we will have to learn to remember them.

---

1 NB. For the way in which 'Law' and 'Right' are used through this text, see the Translator's Note.

1

NOMOS

§1. Isonomia. Tradition has forgotten Cleisthenes; of all the great 'legislators' of ancient Greece, however, he is doubtless the one whose decisions have produced the most serious consequences – and have enjoyed the most enduring legacy. Unlike his predecessors Draco or Solon, he left just a spectre of his existence; we know of his life only through Herodotus' account – and of his laws only through the criticisms of his opponents. But it is a spectre that has forever haunted the history of Europe, as though, at a moment that was as crucial as it was unexpected, it had bestowed on it the decisive direction towards what, for modern man, it was destined to become. When we speak of Greek 'democracy', of the political moment when, suddenly, a new concept bursts into the history of governance and breaks the old equilibrium of aristocracies, it is really of Cleisthenes that we are speaking. Because it was Cleisthenes who, in order to block the attempt to establish an oligarchy in Athens after the tyrant Hippias had been forced out at the beginning of the fifth century BCE, decided, for the first time, to call on the *demos*. Where the former equilibrium had been based on a familial logic, in order to reform the city's institutions so that no tyranny could ever return, Cleisthenes chose to embrace a geographical logic. Until then, Athens had been governed primarily by the aristocratic members of the four major Ionian tribes; from now on, it would be governed by the inhabitants of the one hundred 'demes' into which he divided the city's territory. To this new equilibrium, the name '*isonomia*' was given – equality in the attribution to each of the share to which they were entitled in the city's governance, guaranteed by the institutions that Cleisthenes had created to this end. We should even, perhaps, be more precise: *isonomia* did not just define a form of equality in the attribution of stakes; most importantly, it defined a form of equality before the instrument of this attribution. An instrument for which Cleisthenes invented the name, at the same time that he revealed, through the reforms he conducted with its support, the principles that governed it – the name '*nomos*', the name of 'Law'.

*

§2. *Thesmos.* Contrary to a common misconception, the invention in Greece of what we still call 'Law' was a phenomenon as belated as it was localized – a kind of exotic singularity, belonging to Cleisthenes' reforms. Before them (before, say, 507–506 BCE), no one in the Greek world had ever paid sustained attention to the word '*nomos*', or imagined that it could signify something like a 'Law'. This is not to say that the word was unknown: a great variety of usages have been noted, going back to Hesiod (it does not exist in Homer) and encompassing a large proportion of ancient Greek literature, extending to Pindar and Aeschylus. Notwithstanding this diversity of usage, however, none implied the very peculiar form of normativity that has habitually been associated with the idea of 'Law', and which Cleisthenes helped instigate. Before his intervention, the Greeks were not familiar with the idea of 'Law'; they knew only a constrained form of decision or commandment which they called '*thesmos*' – 'that which is posited'. When, a century before Cleisthenes, Solon recalled the decisions he had made during his archonship, congratulating himself on the wisdom they demonstrated, he did not employ the word '*nomos*', but rather '*thesmos*'. It would have been absurd to consider the matter any further: since Homer, this was the word that had been used to refer to the results of the political activity of the city's leaders inasmuch as it was a matter of an activity focused on *positing something.* As Émile Benveniste once noted, the Indo-European root *dhè– (which is also found in ancient India, in words such as *dharma* and *dhaman*) indicates the foundation, establishment in existence. But this foundation and this establishment never operate generally; they cannot be dissociated from the place [*lieu*] in which they operate – you only posit in the setting [*milieu*] of that which posits: *thesmos* is both the posited *and* that which posits. Neither Law nor constitution, it is *institution* in the most original, elementary and rigorous sense; it is the *fiat* by which what did not exist suddenly appears in the world, finally obtaining the existence that, until then, it lacked.

*

§3. Rhêtra. Nothing was more opposed to the idea of institution than the idea of 'Law', than the word *'nomos'* that Cleisthenes had made the cornerstone of his reforms: in no sense did 'Law', as he conceived it, aim to 'institute'. But neither did it aim to 'constitute', in the sense that it would have sought to provide the city with something like a charter summarizing the fundamental principles governing its operation. The Greeks had a separate word for this too: the word *'rhêtra'* – or the 'thing said' (*rhêtra* is linked to the verb 'to say', *rhêto*), that which has been pronounced once and for all, and to which it is no longer necessary to return. It was a word occurring even more rarely than the word *'nomos'*, and seems only to be confirmed in the case of the Spartan 'constitution', as discussed by Plutarch in the *Life of Lycurgus* (VI, 1–3) – which may have been authored by Lycurgus. The 'Great Rhetra', as Plutarch called it, took the form of an oracle given by the Apollo of Delphi, which Lycurgus was said to have taken back to Sparta, to make it the foundational text on which to base the order of the city. In contrast to *thesmos*, which depended, so to speak, on the demiurgic power of the individual delivering it, *rhêtra* enjoyed a privileged link with the world of the gods – coming, as it did, from the mouth of one of them. The order of the city discovered in the divine order a kind of indirect origin, which conferred on it a 'sacred' dimension – an extraordinary quality establishing the rules by which it was defined in a dimension no longer accessible to everyone. It was no longer a question of a singular *fiat*, the work of a 'thesmothete' like Solon; but rather of a normative emanation of the divine, for which the legislator was just a humble spokesperson, bound by it like everyone else. When he decided to establish a form of *isonomia* in Athens, however, this was not what Cleisthenes was thinking: the *nomoi* he passed were claimed to be neither the emanation of another order, nor the simple result of a legislator's desire. Cleisthenes had a completely different conception of 'Law' in mind, one where the main player in the legislative act would no longer be a god or a legislator, *but the city itself.*

*

§4. *Nemô.* Along with the idea of 'Law', there also
appeared in Greece the idea that the decisions taken by
the leaders of the city required justification – a justification that did not simply take the form of a short circuit
with the divine world. The word '*nomos*' itself conveys
the different significations that its history has introduced
into it, all of which turn around what we might refer
to as 'measurement'. *Nomos* comes from metrology:
it deals with the weighing of rights and duties within
the city, just as, in music, it could signify the temporal
unity with which participants must coordinate in order
to play together. Because the 'measurement' in question
is a *shared* [*partagée*] measurement – as suggested by
the Indo-European root **nem*, from which the verb
nemô, meaning 'to distribute' (which gives us '*nomos*'),
is, it would seem, derived. A measurement that was not
shared would not be a measurement; it would be a kind
of hapax, an incomparable singularity, incommensurable
with any other, as arbitrary and without justification as a
caprice. The irruption of the word '*nomos*' into political
and juridical discourse signals, therefore, the inauguration
of an *order of measurement*, of a shared mechanism that
would at last allow for the *measurement of measurements*.
Nomos is what allocates to each the share to which they
are entitled, the sum of which establishes the sharing of
the city; it is the medium for ordering the order specific
to the city, and of what is shared there. When he sought
to institute *isonomia* in Athens, Cleisthenes did not intend
anything but this: to confer on each their share – or to
ensure that everyone received their due in the order of Law.
Isonomia was the equality of Law and equality before the
Law; it announced that from now on there would be a rule
shared by all, and no longer only the unilateral imposition
of the will of a few. This is the reason why many have seen
here the first democratic moment of ancient Greece – and,
to the extent that we continue to believe in the 'Law', in
nomos, it is a moment that is still today our legacy.

*

§5. *Philosophy.* A banal observation: the philosophical tradition followed immediately in the steps of Cleisthenes and his reforms, producing countless meditations on the theme of *nomos*, which we still read today. The best known of these are by Plato and Aristotle – but they are incomprehensible if we do not keep in mind that they were conceived in response to theories produced by the Sophists. In fact, at the beginning of the fifth century BCE in Athens, the debate on the nature of *nomos* gave tangible form to the fault line that for a long time would delineate the opposition between philosophy and its outside. The nature of this outside is at first difficult to define – but we can say that, in the Sophists, it finds an incarnation through which it can be approached. Were they politicians, lawyers, lecturers or jurists? Maybe a bit of all at once; what is certain, however, is that, in contrast to the philosophers, the Sophists seemed to think that the invention of *nomos* brought little change to the order of the city. The invention of 'Law' was little more than a civilized, polite and dressed-up version of something the inhabitants of Athens had always respected without question – namely, custom, tradition or practice. If Plato and Aristotle decided to follow the change in political vocabulary put forward by Cleisthenes, each in his own way seeking to establish its meaning, it was because they thought otherwise. The order of the city could not be left to customs, traditions or practices, even if its administration should somehow find in them something like an origin or a limit. Be it Plato or Aristotle, after Cleisthenes' reforms, the philosophers all moved in the same direction: what interested them most in the concept of *nomos* was not variability, but permanence. For Greek philosophy, the innovation introduced by the idea of 'Law' was not only that an order existed, but that this order found all the justification it needed in itself. The order, in other words, before being the result of the imposition of a force on the population, and before being a collection of principles enacting its inequitable division, was an *idea*.

*

§6. *Order.* The first to have made the ideal nature of the concept of *nomos* perceptible was doubtless Heraclitus, one of whose fragments took up the connection that, according to him, existed between human *nomos* and divine *nomos*. This connection was not one of participation, as might have been the case with the Great Rhetra of Sparta; it was a connection rooted more in analogy, in a structural relationship between the two forms of *nomos*. Heraclitus wrote: 'τρέφονται γὰρ πάντες οἱ ἀνθρώπειοι νόμοι ὑπὸ ἑνὸς τοῦ θείου' – that is: 'For, all the *nomoi* of men are nourished by that of the gods.' Unlike the oracle of Apollo brought back to Sparta by Lycurgus, human *nomos* was not the simple word of a god, whose meaning it was then a matter of implementing in the city context. It was in fact the same thing as the divine *nomos*; it was equivalent to it inasmuch as the divine *nomos* was the model of all order, that which embodied the ideal of order – or rather the ideal order. The best proof of this was certainly the fact that Heraclitus spoke of the divine *nomos* in the singular: there was only one divine *nomos*; the divine *nomos* was the one Law, the one order, from which the multiple human *nomoi* drew their inspiration. As many scholars have noted, this analogical relation with the divine *nomos* was, paradoxically, what permitted the claim that human *nomoi* were in no way rooted in the sphere of the sacred. The ideal is not the sacred or the divine; it is that whose transcendental incarnation is sometimes supplied by the sacred and the divine – without ever, for all that, exhausting its structural richness, or even supplying its *terminus ad quem*. In distinguishing between two domains of *nomos*, Heraclitus simply highlighted the existence of two manifestations, among other possible manifestations, of what the idea of order was in the first place: an ideal category. Order was an abstraction; it constituted the regulatory universe within which every concrete 'Law' must take place, and so indicated, by necessity, its eternal form; *order was a category of order.* Following Cleisthenes, this is what Plato and Aristotle effectively countersigned when they decided to adopt the vocabulary he had introduced into Athenian juridical life.

*

§7. Polis. Law is indistinguishable from order; order and Law are one thing, and the word '*nomos*' affirms their irreducible identity, their perfect superposition: Law is Law of order and order is order of Law. This identification of Law with order is what distinguished the word '*nomos*' from the word '*thesmos*', which did not in any way encompass a general dimension of order, but rather a singular dimension of will or force. Legal historians have suggested an explanation for this slow drift towards the acceptance, in Athens, of the generalization and abstraction of Law as order – together with the gradual progress of legislation towards the written form. This explanation goes as follows: as Cleisthenes had intended, the development of a logic of order was a way of withdrawing jurisdiction over disputes from the great families, so that it could be handed over to the city. Indeed, for a long time, the resolution of disputes had been the recognized competence of all those in a position to judge, on a case-by-case basis, between the opposing parties. Anyone who had a degree of authority (based on their age, reputation or the simple choice of the parties involved) could play this kind of mediating role, without having to make clear the reasons for the decision they made. In the age of *nomos*, on the other hand, the power to establish Laws and protect order would no longer belong to the great families, nor even to the leaders of the city, but to the city itself, by means of its institutions. Rather than an imprecise and uncertain bundle of decisions, it was now necessary for the state of the legislation in force to be verifiable – singular and concrete forms that could be apprehended in the general and abstract form of order. But this verification could only exist insofar as control of what order meant was taken away from just anybody (namely the citizens) and given over to something transcending

them (namely the City, the *polis*). The rule of Law, as the rule of order, was therefore the rule of the City; it was the City considered as such, which is to say as superior to its citizens, that established the true meaning of the structural abstraction of order.

*

§8. Thémis. In fact, gathering in a single conceptual gesture the ideas of Law, order and City was a radical departure from the conception the Greeks had had, until that time, of order. If, as Benveniste maintained, the concept of order belonged to the most elementary and most fundamental register of Indo-European vocabulary, then their very language was marked by it. The root *ar–*, found in a whole series of Greek locutions (like *arariskô*, to adjust, to harmonize), and which suggested the idea of articulation, adjustment, sequencing [*ordonnancement*], opened a first path. But it was another root, belonging to the same linguistic constellation, that was, according to Benveniste, to prove decisive: the root *dhè–*, of which we have already spoken in the context of *thesmoi*. *Thesmos* was not, in fact, the decision of just any leader; in ancient Greece, it was the measure decreed by the one who, as the head of a family, a *genos*, warranted the title 'themiste'. This was a bifid title: on the one hand, the one who had the power to deliver *thesmoi* was considered a 'themiste'; but, on the other, this power flowed from a superior power, which was called '*thémis*'. The concept of *thémis* has most commonly been translated as 'justice' – but the 'justice' in question had nothing to do with the kind of ethical value the concept has come to embody. It was a question of the 'justice' of the home, of the family, of the *genos* – of 'justice' as a characteristic feature of the order of the home, as opposed to that which does not participate in it, and is of the order of *dikè*. 'Justice' was the quality proper to the *genos*, which, because it was under his direction, was also guaranteed by the 'themiste'; it was the quality of the fact that the family existed – and that

this family was ordered. But this quality was not abstract; it served to define the singular and concrete group, where the themiste, even though he was its chief, was only a more eminent member. Ultimately, 'justice' indicated nothing other than the 'nature of things' that the law of the family professed to regulate.

*

§9. *Phusis.* When they started to critique the idea of *nomos* in the name of *phusis*, of the 'nature of things', the sin committed by the Sophists was perhaps, therefore, one of excessive nostalgia, or blindness to the changes taking place in front of them. To defend *phusis* against *nomos* was effectively to defend the order of the *genos* against the order of the *polis*, the concrete order of the family against the abstract order of the City, by which it had, moreover, been intentionally consigned to history. Indeed, where, in the age of ancient *thémis*, before it became an ethical value, order had been regulated according to criteria coming from a reality external to what was to be regulated, it now regulated itself. *Nomos* had become its own regulation, since the order that had produced it was precisely the one it was establishing, and for which it was claiming to define the programme – at the same time as it was defined by it. There was something closed, shut off, tautological, in the establishment of the idea of Law: the tautology that always accompanies an abstraction when it seeks to constitute its own stratum of reality. It was this tautology that the Sophists (with Protagoras first in line) attempted to critique through recourse to *phusis*, without grasping the desperate nature of this attempt. The order of *nomos* was of such novelty that everything based in a former configuration had lost all purchase on it – this being precisely what it wanted to rid itself of. It was pointless to confront it with the necessity of rediscovering the concrete ground of the judicial decision, of reconciling itself with the familial unity of the former jurisdiction, or of taking up again a thesmotic conception of regulation. From the

moment it became a question of smashing the former
order of justice that the great families had hoped to see
endure, as had been Cleisthenes' goal with his programme
of reforms, it became equally necessary to abandon, or at
least reinvent, all the categories that were rooted in. And
for Cleisthenes, as for Plato and Aristotle, this reinvention
could take but one form: a form, authorized by the
invention of *nomos*, that decisively affirmed the superiority of the City over everything it contained – starting
with the citizens.

*

§*10. Anomia.*   The pre-eminence, in ancient Greece,
of the city over the citizens, of the *polis* over the *politès*,
was not, moreover, a matter of simple chance; it too
belongs, if we are to believe Benveniste, to the very
structure of the Greek language. In the history of the
language's development, he recalls, the word '*politès*'
must be considered a derivation from the word '*polis*' – a
direct linguistic consequence of its establishment. From
the perspective of language, there is no possible '*politès*'
prior to the existence of the *polis*, because the word '*polis*'
is the linguistic kernel of the word '*politès*', which is only
the result of its extension. This means that the citizen,
in ancient Greece, was supplementary to the City; he
was accessory to the essential City; he issued from and
depended on the *polis*, which was 'necessary and sufficient
for defining the *politès*'. Without the City, the citizen,
beneficiary of the rights it accorded him and recipient of
the offices and privileges it bestowed on him, did not exist;
he was just a nameless and unattached individual, drifting
in a hostile, chaotic and dissolute world. To bring order to
the world, and so that the individual could benefit from it,
an entity had to exist through which all order was established – because it constituted its primary embodiment.
But this entity, Benveniste adds, was embodied 'in neither
a structure, nor an institution, nor an assembly'; it was
an 'abstract body', existing by itself, independent of men.

For the Greeks, the city was the abstract idea of order; the city was *nomos*; the city was *archè*, the principle without which everything was in danger of sinking into *anomia*, into illegality, which was also disorder – and vice versa. It is, therefore, as the central category in a political ecology based on abstraction and generalization that we should consider the idea of *nomos*, the Greek invention of 'Law', and its defence by the philosophers. This is particularly troubling as the whole juridical culture of the West has chosen to follow them and to make the idea of *nomos* into a transcendental category serving to articulate its understanding of Right [*droit*]. Just as the pre-eminence of the city over the citizens is still the *motto* of political vocabulary, so, for juridical vocabulary, the omnipotence of Law remains the most indisputable truth.

INTERLUDE 1

§B. *Chaos.* *Anomia* is *an-archè*: the absence of Law is the absence of foundation, principle or rule, understood as the mode of consistency of everything that is – starting with human cities, those dangerously inclined associations. Without *nomos*, the very possibility of justifying the way things are is nullified, along with the possibility of this justification enabling the control of what is considered dangerous – the word for which is chaos. Since the invention of the category of Law in Greece, it has always been brandished as a way of avoiding the chaos that would surely ensue in a society left to its own devices – it being understood that, without a master, men are animals. That the absence of Law and order always leads to chaos is among the least well-founded, but simultaneously most deep-rooted, propositions of the legalistic ethos that has governed the West for more than two millennia. Why? Without doubt because *only* the hypothesis of chaos can, in the struggle for mastery, serve to justify the unjustifiable – can supply a principle or an unquestionable purpose to the category of Law. The hypothesis of chaos is an ace in a game where they are lacking; or rather, it is a *joker*, an empty card that might replace any of them, from the weakest to the strongest, depending on the interests being perused. As such, the card of chaos is without content or power; it is, literally, a *carte blanche*; but it is this absence that allows it to plug the holes in the shaky edifice of Western legalism. Rather than a collection of arguments, therefore, it only works through suggestions: 'it might be that', 'the danger would be', 'but that might leave the door open to', and so on. In other words: the hypothesis of chaos *is* the hypothesis of what these suggestions would give one to believe; it *is* chaos, in the sense that, when it is employed, all consistencies collapse. The hypothesis of chaos is what induces the necessity for worry, doubt and fear, where previously they appeared only as circumstances allowed – since only their necessity also makes it necessary to control them with *nomos*.

2

DĪNUM

§11. Hammurabi. Nearly 1,250 years before Cleisthenes enacted his reforms, Hammurabi, the king of Babylon, ordered the erection of a stele of black basalt in the middle of the court of the temple dedicated to the sun god Šamaš in the city of Sippar. The monument was 2.25 metres high and 55 centimetres across, covered on both sides by a text written in cuneiform characters, and topped with a bas-relief image of the king receiving the insignia of royalty. The first part of the text narrates Hammurabi's achievements over the course of his reign, also recounting the magnanimity he had demonstrated, through his wisdom and his courage, in the exercise of power. The second part, composed of 282 separate sections, is in the form of short scenes outlining the consequences to be expected for some action or other undertaken by an individual. The third part takes the form of a curse on anyone disrespecting the stele's probity, combined with an expression of the hope that its contents will be preserved for eternity – along with the name of the king. When Hammurabi took the decision to order the stele, he was coming to the end of a reign that had lasted around forty years, during which he had made Babylon into the most important kingdom in Mesopotamia. When he came to the throne in 1792 BCE, the city was just one of a number of powers, forced to coexist with several threatening neighbours governed by other kings of the Amorite dynasty: Larsa, Eshnunna or Mari. Forty years later, thanks to the skilful military campaigns of its sovereign, Babylon had been able to defeat its neighbours, extending its empire along the whole length of the Tigris and the Euphrates, to the edge of Mesopotamia. More than Hammurabi's exploits, however, the text engraved on the stele emphasized the *way* in which they had been achieved, and the virtues the king had evinced in the accomplishment of his tasks. Among these virtues, there was one that, because it announced his divine election, was to be placed above all the others: the virtue of *šar mišarim* – of being 'king of justice'.

*

§12. Mišarum. In the Babylonian tradition, a king's greatness was judged on the proximity of his relationship with the gods, the proof of which came less from his successes than from the evidence of their inspiration. And the place where this inspiration was most in evidence was in the sphere of justice, understood not as the art of deciding, but as the spectacle of mastery in matters of fairness. In fact, justice, *mišarum*, implied much more than a simple judicial performance; it was a demonstration of the 'restoration of equity', the re-establishment of the equilibrium that had been broken by the action of an individual. One technique the king could use to accomplish this restoration was, literally, to declare it through the 'edicts of grace' ('*mišarum*', again), cancelling all debts. But while these edicts could be enacted at the beginning of a reign to authorize the return to an as yet undisturbed situation, to turn to them subsequently constituted a new rupture. In normal times, *mišarum* just looked like banal judicial procedures, which it was in the king's gift to decide in the form of lapidary vocal proclamations made during public hearings. These judgements claimed to be '*awāt mišarim*' ('word of justice') or '*dīnāt mišarim*' ('judgement of justice') – expressions that figure prominently in the third part of the text of Hammurabi's stele. It is in fact among the *dīnum*, the 'judgements', 'trials' or 'cases', that the brief stories making up most of the inscriptions engraved in the basalt should be counted. The 282 scenes that can be read there represent so many decisions made by Hammurabi, of which he was sufficiently proud to want to hand them down to posterity. Each of them embodied a moment of divine inspiration, crystallized as an exercise in fairness where the king himself, as the guardian of the existing state of affairs, was the only expected beneficiary. The text of the stele is open about this, and speaks of them as his *awātiya šūqurātim*, his 'precious words'.

*

§13. Dīnum. When, in Susa in 1902, the stele was exhumed during a French archaeological expedition directed by the explorer Jacques de Morgan, these 'words' were puzzling to the specialists who accompanied him. In the edition of the engraved text produced the following year for the *Mémoires de la délégation de Perse*, the reverend father Jean-Vincent Scheil, seeking to dispel any doubts, decided to view it as a 'code'. Even if the interpretation was, to say the least, primitive, its success was proportionate to the discovery, and the monument, stored at the Louvre, is still today known as the 'Code of Hammurabi'. In truth, before we are able speak of a 'code', certain formal and material elements must come together – elements that are not present in the text found on the stele. In addition to the *codex* form (which did not appear until the second century BCE in Rome), we would also expect to be able to detect a minimum level of systemization, generalization and abstraction – which is not the case. Instead, Hammurabi's *awātiya* appear as a loose and disordered collection, exploring, sometimes excessively, even inconsistently, a range of hypotheses that are as arbitrary as they are limited. The text of the 'Code', moreover, explicitly uses a particular word to refer to itself: *'dīnum'* – a word that also serves to refer to each item, each of the 'cases' or 'trials' making up the long central section. Just as justice, *mišarum*, meant both the value of equity and the instrument through which it was to be carried out, *dīnum* meant casuistry as much as the case, the verdict as much as the collection of verdicts that had been given. To speak of a 'code', therefore, is to miss the essential aspect of Hammurabi's *dīnum*: the fact that it provides a shorthand for a general casuistry, whose movement encompasses the totality of the activity of *mišarum*. Justice, in Babylon, was nothing but the sum of the judgements by which the king had resolved the trials brought before him – or rather had employed the wisdom of a principle of equity thought to have settled them since time immemorial.

*

§14. Šumma. This singular relationship with time is apparent in the fact that, rather than being presented as a conclusive decision, each *dīnum* takes the form of a kind of general declaration, seemingly disconnected from the case that instigated it. Each judgement is expressed in two stages, the first introduced by the word *šumma* ('if', 'supposing that', 'being that'), presenting in the present the hypothesis in question, and the second drawing a conclusion conjugated in the future. 'If someone (a free man) captures a runaway male or female slave in the open country and returns them to their master,' says, for example, *dīnum* 17, 'the master of the slave will give him two shekels of silver.' The reason for the recourse to this protasis and apodosis form stems partly from the structure of Sumerian languages, and partly from the way in which this was deployed in a context like that of justice. Unlike other dialects belonging to the group of Indo-European languages, Akkadian contained no words for expressing the deontic nuances of duty or capacity – it did not know the idea of norm. This does not mean that it was unaware of the possibility of moving from one state of affairs to another, with the latter considered as resulting necessarily from the former; it was content to formulate this necessity by other means. These means being precisely the protasis and apodosis structure – a structure over which Hammurabi's 'precious words' did not have a monopoly, since it is found in all the principal genres of Babylonian literature. It is, notably, the defining trait of a considerable collection of texts, the oldest of which significantly predate the time when the 'Code' was written: the collection of divinatory tracts. Like Hammurabi's *dīnum*, these tracts were composed of verses divided into protasis and apodosis, with a view to extracting the necessary consequence from a factual hypothesis – which it was therefore permitted to declare. This is hardly surprising, since among the different meanings of the word '*dīnum*', there is one that corresponds perfectly to this use: that of 'prophesy' or 'prediction'.

*

§15. *Prophesy.* The contents of the Babylonian divinatory tracts brought to light through archaeological research do indeed display the same stylistic traits and the same syntactical structure as the *dīnum* of Hammurabi's 'Code'. 'If a man with a flushed face has his right eye protruding: far from home, the dogs will devour him', prophesizes one of these tracts in the same way as the 'Code' might proclaim a sanction. In both cases, we are dealing with a *dīnum*, which is to say a verdict bound to the inevitable nature of the consequence following an observed situation – an inevitability presented as the specific knowledge that prophecy reveals. In fact, as Jean Bottéro has demonstrated, the divinatory tracts are also situated in a much larger epistemological universe, encompassing the whole of the 'scientific' knowledge developed by Babylonian scholars. Whether dealing with medicine or mathematics, the reasoning found in scientific tracts is identical to that found in divinatory tracts. The protasis and apodosis structure formed the very structure of the relation to the world that, according to the Babylonians, knowledge could uncover: a structure based on the absolute necessity of what happens. *There is only prophetic knowledge* – this is the maxim that implicitly governed the Babylonian way of seeing the world, from the moment that, hypothetically, it came to be based on a general principal of necessity. The divinatory tracts were the exemplary form of this knowledge, which the other kinds of 'science' found themselves compelled to imitate if they wanted to share in its explanatory, and therefore predictive, properties. Judicial science was no exception: it also belonged to the sphere of expanded divination, as a means of access to a better understanding of the world and its order. Such that, for Hammurabi, the proclamation of a *dīnum* did not only demonstrate moral knowledge, but also a true knowledge of the principles on which the order of the world was purported to be based. Justice, *mišarum*, was only virtuous to the extent that it was knowledge, and it was only knowledge to the extent that it was virtuous.

*

§16. *Šamaš.* *To judge is to predict*; it is not to decide on the possible application of a norm to an actual situation, it is to prophesize the necessary occurrence of a consequence following a particular event; it is not to determine, it is to know. Beyond the formal identity of reasoning styles, there are other elements that allow us to argue for the close relationship between judicial and divinatory practices in Babylon. The first is the recourse to the same logical methods of exploration as casuistry; in the divinatory tracts, as in the 'codes', a method of variation could be used to refine hypotheses. This procedure consisted of adding new conditions to existing conditions, so that a different prophesy could be extracted, as the *dīnum* opening the 'Code' of Hammurabi which deals with the case of accusation demonstrates. 'If someone has accused a man, charging him with murder, but has been unable to prove it, the accuser shall be put to death', says the text in a variation on another *dīnum* stipulating that, 'If a man has committed a murder, the man will be killed'. Rather than the systematicity of an abstract cartography, the method of variations enabled the elaboration of a casuistic tree, authorizing all permutations of the branches that made up the original hypothesis. The essential thing, in any case, was not to get to the point where, by this method, the whole range of possible scenarios had been exhausted; instead, it was a question of recognizing how the world itself appeared to the understanding. For the Babylonians, the world was not to be explained, since this explanation found everything it needed in the activity of the gods, but to be described, and divination and judgement were two forms of description. But that is not all: as well as the proximity of forms and methods, we should also note that Hammurabi had erected the stele to his glory in the enclosure of a temple dedicated to Šamaš. Now, the role attributed to Šamaš in Babylonian mythology goes beyond being the embodiment of the sun's light; as 'master of judgement and decision' (*bēl dīnum u purussim*), he was also the god of divination.

*

§17. Kittum. That Šamaš could be, at the same time, the god of illumination, divination and judgement is explained by the unity of the operation that these three perform: the operation of understanding – the elucidation of the world. If judging equates to predicting, then judging also means knowing, illuminating in the omnipotence of daylight that which sought to remain hidden in the shadows, but which was part of the way things were. That was what the god was handing down to Hammurabi in the bas-relief at the top of the stele: in giving him the instruments of royalty, the ring and the baton, he was presenting him with the instruments of understanding. Because, in Babylonian symbolism, the purpose of the ring and the baton was not to signify prestige; they represented the function they were believed to fulfil, namely measurement and the ability to draw straight lines. Thanks to the ring, it was possible to calculate the area of fields or to determine the foundations of buildings; using the baton, it was possible to draw rectilinear sections and to establish precisely their length. It was, therefore, the way in which Hammurabi managed, using the instruments of power, to deploy the principle of understanding whose divine form was embodied in Šamaš, that confirmed that he had been elected by the gods. In other words: what the god was giving to the king went beyond a few useful tools; what he was giving was himself – the light of the sun, as a source of knowledge about the constitution of the world. From the moment he became the custodian of such knowledge, Hammurabi no longer needed to decide or to legislate; law or decision only making sense where ignorance reigns, his practice of justice could ignore what ought to be. *Mišarum* was nothing like a regulatory norm or a supreme principle towards which the actions of the population were to be orientated; it was rather the sign of the successful confirmation of a state of affairs. This state of affairs was called '*kittum*' in the 'Code': 'the public order as just, as solid' – which is to say, as given, as amenable to an understanding where predictions can be established, and not as something to respect.

*

§18. Model. Hammurabi's decision to erect a stele in the temple of Šamaš in Sippa, and then to have multiple copies of it sculpted in other parts of his kingdom, should be understood according to the same logic. Finding himself invested with the principle embodied by the god, the king acted in direct conformity with him; he was not inspired by him, he imitated him, in the most consistent sense of the term; he accomplished what Šamaš accomplished. The writing up of a choice of *dīnum* belonged to this logic of imitation, since it also represented a way in which the king could transmit his deed by way of an agent other than himself – an agent endowed with his prerogative. Such that, as Dominique Charpin emphasizes, its true efficacity was to be found in its simple presence, the reminder of the existence of a principle of justice of which the king had the highest knowledge. The different steles distributed to all corners of the kingdom did not represent so many attempts to publicize the text of the 'laws' that the citizens were supposed to obey; their role was to be there, just like the world itself. The best proof of this is that, even though the 'Code' was copied many times in the millennium following its composition (the most recent copies dating from the seventh century BCE), no official citation has ever been found. In their imitative activity of the king's justice, the judges had no need to turn to the sentences that appeared there, since it was not so much the contents of the 'Code' that was important, but the principle it applied. The 'Code' was a *model* that only constituted a reference as a 'tract on the exercise of judicial power', as Jean Bottéro put it – as the summation of an art for which the sentences should be taken as evidence. This does not mean that no 'norms' existed in Babylon, or that they could not be employed; it means only that they played no role *vis-à-vis* a principle that bestowed its greatness on the action of judging. It was to this principle that the judges turned to justify their own judgements – a principle appearing under the generic form of a recourse to the 'decisions of the king' (*simdāt sārrim*), without further detail.

*

§19. Akālum. The fact that something like juridical 'normativity' was part of the daily reality of Babylonian Right [*droit*] is confirmed by the existence of a significant body of contract forms discovered between 1934 and 1938 in the palace of the ancient city of Mari. Before the kingdom was conquered by Hammurabi in 1760 BCE, the scribes employed a range of contractual templates enabling them to guarantee sound relations between the counterparties in a transfer of goods. The way in which this guarantee was established through a contract of this kind was not, however, based on a form of obligation that was in any way comparable to the one that would come into existence more than a millennium later in Rome. Rather than a juridical bond, the forms provided for the fulfilment of certain actions, such as the presence of one or several witnesses – who might themselves be required to carry out a ritual action. Among these actions, the most significant concerned the fact of 'eating' ('*akālum*'), where the object to be ingested could just as well be 'bread' ('*ninda*') or an 'oath' ('*nīsam*'). That an oath could be eaten (which is to say that a little cursed food was ingested, which, in an instance of perjury, would release its curse) already indicates that the relationship established by this kind of 'contract' was anything but mandatory. Instead of an obligatory bond, the form constituted an experimental protocol to which the counterparties agreed to subject themselves, knowing that each of them would be altered by it. The forms did not bind, they noted the results of an experiment: like the 'Code', they belonged to a logic for which the 'norm' did not exist except as a fact, except as a more or less objective description of a situation. Just as the Akkadian language possessed no deontic operator, Babylonian juridical thought resisted any conception of the obligatory, the normative or the legal; it conceived only of cases and actions. Even outside the shadow of a 'Code', the scribes practised a Right that refused to develop within a horizon structured by what ought to be: their Right existed only as an anti-Right, as a negative Right.

*

§20. Understanding. The Mesopotamia of the era of the Amorite dynasty was no exception; all the other documents in our possession indicate that the factual logic shaping Babylonian 'Right' was very widely shared. In the years following the exhumation of the stele of Hammurabi's 'Code', other compilations of sentences were discovered in the region, some dating from 2100 BCE. Despite temporal and geographic differences, they share the same characteristics: casuistic logic, the protasis and apodosis structure, recourse to a method of variation, the absence of a deontic operator. For more than 1,500 years the Right of the Middle East, from Sumer to Babylon, from Assyria to the Hittite empire, was based on a relation to the world that had no recourse to the idea of norm. Without knowing it, this was the relation to the world that, despite the desperate attempt instigated by the Sophists to rescue *physis*, the Greek invention of *nomos* consigned to the dustbin of history. With it, the possibility of imagining Right within a horizon other than that of 'Law' was lost for a long time; from then on, Right no longer had any claim to the status of instrument of understanding. On the contrary, it was from a place of ignorance that it was now to be deployed – the task of knowing finding itself delegated to those in possession of instruments enabling the understanding of the concept of *nomos*, namely the philosophers. Babylon did not need philosophers, just as it did not need jurists; instead, the soothsayers and the scribes, two categories of individual who knew that knowledge was situated here below, took on all the work. The rupture introduced by the idea of *nomos* was not, therefore, only a rupture with the very conception (or possibility) of Right; it was also a rupture with what served as the source of knowledge. To turn to *nomos* was to recognize that nothing belonging to the world of man could serve as true knowledge; this, if it existed, meant redirecting your gaze to more ethereal spheres – in Right as in everything else.

INTERLUDE 2

§C. *Code.* In the history of Western Right, codification is still presented as the high point of a long process of rationalization, culminating in the perfection of a systematic organization of social relations. The code, as a formal instrument, establishes the ordering of the technic of order that is Law – its extension within a rational reading of the world, that the systematization of the code is supposed to authorize. In order for the jump from fact to Right to take place, there must exist a mode of representation that accepts both a separation with the factual reality of the world and a formal harmonization with its mode of operation. In itself, Law remains powerless to offer such a mode of representation; its desire for order still belonging to the register of appeal, of invocation or conjuration – the register of rhetoric. With the code, rhetoric becomes aesthetic: the stylistics of Law becomes a machinery of perception, whose logical artifice, based on the arborescent model developed in the natural sciences, speaks the truth. The code offers a landscape in which the perfection of relations between rule and exception, and the exhaustive complexity of branches and distinctions can be taken to describe the *normative reality* of the world. Along with factual reality, there exists, by virtue of the existence of Law and the deontic machinery that comes with it, a normative reality – a reality of the obligations constitutive of every human connection. The central hypothesis of every code is essentially that every relation to some degree belongs to the sphere of obligations: every relation is made up of rights and obligations, for which the operational conditions are determined by way of Law. It is on this hypothesis that the ordering of the world performed by the code is based – and Law needs it if it is to exceed the restrictive borders of sovereign command and caprice. With the code, contrary to a still common belief, it is not the code that demands: it is the world itself – in that the code expresses the structure of its fundamental order, given in a multitude of relations. A structure that is not to be known but obeyed.

3

IUS

§21. Rogatio. The way in which the Greek invention of
nomos closed off the juridical age of the model should be
understood as an unprecedented theoretical takeover, the
objective of which was the supervision of Right by Law.
Given that a good deal of its development was based on
an oblique glance in the direction of the neighbouring
culture, it is all the more surprising to note that the
Roman world resisted this supervision. In the accounts
that have been preserved on the adoption of the *Lex
Duodecim Tabularum*, the 'Law of the Twelve Tables', the
most venerable document of the Roman legal tradition,
this glance took on material form in expeditions. Livy,
Dionysius of Halicarnassus and Diodorus Siculus all give
the same account: Rome was shaken by conflicts between
patricians and plebeians over their power with respect to
one another; taking advantage of the absence of consuls
away at war, Caius Terentilius Harsa, the tribune of the
plebs, suggested in 462 BCE that a *rogation* in his name
be adopted, with the aim of putting into writing the
obscure rules employed by the consuls. This was a failure.
Some years later, the plebeians called for the writing of
an agrarian law effecting a fair distribution of the lands
conquered by the armies of the Republic, which were
mostly made up of members of their class. In the face of
patrician resistance, the plebeians were obliged to resort
to force in order to obtain, in 452, the appointment of
a commission of ten exceptional consuls, responsible for
the composition of a kind of 'code' of Laws applicable to
everyone. According to the accounts of Roman historians,
this commission went to make enquiries with Greece
(either continental Greece or, as seems more likely, the
Greek colonies in the south of the Italian peninsula), to
find out how they had resolved the issue. The ten consuls
returned with a number of measures, which were carved
into wooden tablets and made public – measures grouped
into ten, and then twelve, sections, each dedicated to
a particular subject. For the first time, Rome had at its
disposal a body of written rules, which anyone could
know, regardless of their social status or class.

*

§22. *Ius.* In fact, when Latin historians came to recount
the history of the *Lex*, a long time had already passed since
its adoption – and, most importantly, since the transformation of Roman legal sensitivities. In the first century
BCE, the Roman intellectual world had succumbed in its
entirety to the view that true greatness was to be found
in Greece, and that theirs was the only philosophy worth
the effort. Even though the Law of the Twelve Tables was
still considered a decisive element in the elaboration of
Roman Right, from then on it found itself interpreted
according to a narrative enabling the establishment of a
continuity with the Greek world. For Livy, the *decemviri*
of the commission responsible for the writing down of
Roman Law had found their initial inspiration in the laws
(*thesmoi*) decreed in Athens by Solon in 594 BCE. But this
was to directly exclude the most original feature of the
Lex: the fact that the body of rules it announced explicitly
referred to a concept that Solon could not have known
– the Latin concept of *ius*. The most important thing
achieved by the *Lex* was the putting into writing of *ius*, of
the 'Right' applying to plebeians, for which the different
rules it formulated were only an appearance, as contingent
as it was arbitrary. In the past, the pontifical authorities,
who were then in charge of justice, had adopted a number
of solutions, resulting in very specific formulas – but these
formulas in no way exhausted the meaning of *ius*. It was
difficult, moreover, to give it a positive definition; the
supplement that *ius* represented with respect to *leges* was
close to being inexpressible – a reality so self-evident that
it required no clarification. Even if *ius* did not exist outside
the different formulas assembled in the twelve tables of
the *Lex*, this existence was not fully expressed there; it
was *something other* than the formulas and rules that they
articulated. The problem was that this 'something other'
had nothing to do with the meaning the Greeks had given
to the *thesmoi* or *nomoi* their legislators had adopted; the
concept of *ius* owed them nothing – nothing at all.

*

§23. *Fas*. In order to understand the singularity of Roman *ius*, it is no doubt necessary to go back before the proclamation of the Law of the Twelve Tables to focus on the reasons why, to start with, it was a prerogative of the pontiffs. Besides their authority in the sphere of the observance of religious rites, the reading of omens and supervision of the maintenance of the Pons Sublicius over the Tiber, they were indeed responsible for administering justice. The way they went about it was, however, very particular: to approach the pontiffs with a view to asserting a right meant setting in motion a machine that might well destroy the one activating it. If you wanted to initiate legal proceedings, you had to start by choosing the 'legal formula' appropriate to the case, and by delivering it without making a mistake under penalty of dismissal. If one word was missed or mistaken, or if the formula chosen was not the right one, this was enough for the case to be closed immediately, with no chance of appeal – while the appropriate formula, delivered correctly, meant things could move forward. To take legal action in the time of the pontiffs was to submit yourself to a kind of trial by ordeal, involving the mobilization of forces far surpassing the limits of a simple citizen, and to which it was advisable to address yourself according to the rules. In fact, legal activity in ancient Rome was an activity that, while distinct from what at the time was called '*fas*' (what we might call 'the sacred'), belonged, nonetheless, to the same ecology. This was an ecology of the sacred word, inasmuch as it demonstrated a particular effective capacity – simply speaking, it produced an effect that was impossible to escape. Choosing a formula in the context of a legal proceeding was, therefore, like saying a kind of prayer, which, if uttered in exactly the right way, was expected to force the powers it called on to intervene to settle the case in question. So, the expected effects did not so much concern the counterparties in the proceedings as it did the forces in a position to assure the result – forces that needed *conjuring*.

*

§24. *Iura.* In ancient Roman Right, *iurare* did not,
therefore, mean 'to express Right [*droit*]' but 'to say the
correct prayer', or 'use the correct conjuring formula', in
order that it produce its expected effects. *Ius* was inscribed
in the linguistic regime of the oath, understood as a
procedure through which supra-terrestrial powers were
summoned to assure the truth of a declaration or promise.
To seek to conjure them through the utterance of an *iura*
such as could be read in the *Lex Duodecim Tabularum*
was to take an oath, this being also understood as a
kind of performative prayer. Playing the role of witness
to this conjuration, the *iudex*, or judge, simply approved
or disapproved the choice of the formula the appellant
had decided to use. He 'expressed' Right in the sense that
he indicated the appropriate *iura*, that he identified the
correct formula – the one, that is, where it was possible
to hope for the effects sought when the decision to visit
the *iudex* had been taken. But he decided nothing, since
what was in question in the cases presented to him was the
responsibility of those calling on him; he was nothing but
the intermediary between them and the forces they wanted
to set in motion. Likewise, the proper register for the *iura*
was not the normative, an ought entailing that those to
whom they addressed themselves should comply more or
less voluntarily, more or less loosely. Once the appropriate
formula had been uttered, a necessity much greater than
that of a deontic was activated – a necessity that no desire
or ploy could circumvent. Rather than to the normative
register, *ius* belonged to the imperative, as illustrated by
the grammatical structure of the *iura*, always constructed
in the manner of an injunction, commandment or direct
order – and not a duty. Compliance with the content of
a formula was never in question in Roman Right; once
the *ius* had been indicated, it was considered to enter into
effect ineluctably, like destiny, like *fas*, whose world it
shared.

*

§25. Nexum. Table VI of the *Lex*, devoted to goods, shows most clearly how '*ius*' should be understood; its first *iura*, as related by Festus, stipulates: '*cum nexum faciet mancipiumque, uti lingua nuncupassit, ita ius esto.*' Literally translated, this reads something like: 'when someone makes a *nexum* or a mancipation, and declares it by word of mouth (orally), it shall be right (*ius*).' By this, we should understand that the recognition of the expected effectiveness of a *nexum* or a mancipation came about through the conclusion of oral formalities, with the *iura* instructing that they had the ability to produce this result. In any case, the putting into servitude of the one who did not fulfil their obligation was declared to flow necessarily from the carrying out of the relevant formalities, along with the saying of certain words. The formalities in question were those said to be '*per aes et libram*', 'by the as [a bronze coin] and scales', namely the taking in hand of a certain quantity of money and a set of scales, which had to be held while the ritual words were pronounced. If the gestures and the words were properly enacted, then the *nexum* or the mancipation automatically produced their effect, which the Romans named '*damnatio*', 'damnation'. It was this 'damnation' of the debtor, guaranteeing the payment of his debt by means of the promise of his servitude if he failed to honour it, that the *iura* of the Law of the Twelve Tables sanctioned by ordaining that this was really the way things were – that there was really *ius*. This did not therefore take the form of a 'rule of Right' which should have been applied, but of a collection of actions whose realization produced a decisive change in the relations uniting a debtor to his creditor. By deciding to enter into a kind of contract (in fact, the actual idea of a contract did not appear for several centuries after the *Lex* were decreed), the interested parties demonstrated that they were ready to undergo a transformation against which they had no power. Such was the *ius* that the *iura* prescribed: the transformation of a citizen into a debtor destined for servitude if he did not settle his debt.

*

§26. *Civitas.* For the Romans, 'Right' was not a means by which to manage the way things were, but an operator of transformation whose effects were limited to the situations in which it intervened – whether through formulas or by other devices. This meant that Right was the guardian of nothing but an actor in everything; it constituted a mode of intervention in the world, whose effectiveness meant it could add, subtract or modify this or that point at will. As the decision taken to give in to the demands of the plebeians and to have the Law of the Twelve Tables written up shows: the only *iura* that had been collated were those intended to apply to them. There was a whole range of other spheres that did not concern them – just as there were spheres that no *ius* touched, like that which we today call 'public law'. The *ius* of Ancient Rome related only to relations existing between citizens; in no way did it concern those connecting them with the authorities – and, even less, those the authorities cultivated among themselves. This was why it was often referred to as *ius civile*, as in civil law [*droit civil*], as in the rights attached to the quality of citizenship – as though there could be no *ius* without this quality, or one to which another standard could be applied. This 'civil' right was not, however, a 'civic' right; it was a right of the citizens and not a right of the city – in other words: it was a privilege of the subjects, and not a defining characteristic of public order. As Benvenista has shown, in Roman vocabulary, the city (*civis*) is a derivation from citizenship (*civitas*), whereas in Greece the movement went in the opposite direction: in Rome, the citizens make the city, and not the city the citizens. And the same went for Right, which only existed as a transformative tool used by the citizens to alter their particular qualities, to modify their particular situation or status, outside of any public intervention. Even though it came about in a religious context, and its implementation required the intervention of nonhuman forces (albeit unnamed), *ius* had no horizon other than its own efficacy within a network of citizen relations.

*

§27. *Corpus.* Since Roman Right was first and foremost a citizen's Right, the fact that it emerged in the context of the activity of the pontiffs, who all belonged to a defined class in Roman society, should be considered secondary. In the years following the proclamation of the Law of the Twelve Tables, the increasing sophistication of the operational machinery for which it had in a sense set the programme was direct proof of this. Far from being the work of the pontiffs, or of those, like the *praetor urbanus*, who replaced them in the administration of justice from 366 BCE, innovations to *ius* were signed off by ordinary Romans. Neither judges, nor litigants, nor government officials, they were citizens with the time and the means to commit themselves to the study of Right – as they might have done for any other prestigious, quasi-sophisticated hobby. In the milieu of the sixth century BCE, the main categories, institutions, distinctions and operations of *ius civile*, and of the *ius gentium* applicable to relations between citizens and non-citizens, were created by them. Neither the pontiffs nor, following the abandonment of the Formula Procedure for which they were the guardians, the *praetor urbanus* or the *praetor peregrinus* devised the categories through which *ius* created its own reality. They just opened the range of possible formulas to which citizens could turn – but the technical meaning of these new formulas, and their effective applicability, were devised by citizens whose only entitlement was their simple interest in the subject. As the text of the *Corpus Iuris Civilis*, the great systemization ordered by Justinian in 529 CE, attests, the history of Roman Right is, first, the history of these strange enthusiasts. Quintus Mucius, Servius, Labeo, Pomponius, Gaius, etc.: these are the names of those who *fabricated* Roman Right – using the raw, and always changing, materials of pontifical formulas, legal actions, praetorian edicts, etc. It is their words that are related in the *Corpus Iuris Civilis*, summarizing nearly a thousand years of legal innovation – while legislation featured only adventitiously.

*

§28. *Iurisprudentia.* Right is not in the business of
norms, it is in the business of operations; it is not in the
business of legislation, it is in the business of knowledge –
a technical knowledge without which no Law can hope to
be of consequence. In the case of the *nexum* and the mancipation whose formula was advanced in the *Lex Duodecim
Tabularum*, this is the knowledge of what is produced
from the ritual of gestures and words surrounding its realization: obligation. No royal decision, no *iura* of the *Lex*,
and no subsequent edict ever specified what an obligation
was, or why the elaboration of this category constituted
a necessary condition for the efficacy of the institution in
question. It was the patient work of the scholars of *ius*,
the *iurisprudentes*, that extracted the category from the
great variety of formulas and situations, to the extent that
they considered it appropriate to the resolution of the
difficulties presented by a 'contract' like the *nexum* or the
mancipation. The decisive gesture came, in this instance,
from Publius Mucius Scavola in the second century BCE
when he decided to distinguish between the 'real' effect
and the 'obligatory' effect of an agreement – the effect in
the world and the effect on individuals. As opposed to the
mancipation, which involved the actual taking in hand
of the object of the agreement, and therefore the actual
change in its possession, the *nexum* produced an effect on
the counterparties, whom it transformed as such. It was
thanks to the notion of 'obligatory effect' that, a century
later, Servius Sulpicius Rufus was able to gather all the
measures sharing the same logic under the title *contractus*,
'contract'. Without it, traditions as different as *nexum* or
mancipation would have continued to exist separately,
developing in ways that would doubtless have been
entrenched in their differences. Only the learned exercise
of juridical reason to which the lay non-professionals were
devoted meant that things turned out differently, enabling
the introduction into the world of *ius* of a category that
was to overturn the course of human relations. Right's
true source was not to be found in the *iura* of the pontiffs,

the praetorian provisions or senatorial decrees; it was to be found in the science of *iurisprudentia*.

*

§29. *Institutes.* Among the works that left their traces in the *Corpus Iuris Civilis*, just one is preserved in its entirety: the textbook written by Gaius in the middle of the second century under the title *Institutes*, which was borrowed by Justinian to name a section of his summa. Even though it was devised following a plan that sought to group problems and solutions according to their similarities, Gaius's book made no claim to be a complete exposure of what might be considered a system. Rather than a system, the *Institutes* described the infinite derivations that could be explored from a given set of logical distinctions – meaning that it looked more like a collection of hypotheses than anything else. Besides the distinction between *ius gentium* and *ius civile*, the one destined for the greatest success was that by which Gaius separated problems relating to individuals (*personas*), things (*res*) or actions (*actiones*). Similarly, when it came to individuals, the key was to decide on their circumstances: a free man (*liberi*) was to be distinguished from a slave (*servi*) – while, among the freemen, a different fate was reserved for those born free (*ingenui*) and those who had been freed (*libertine*). The branching of distinctions went on in this way before coming to individual situations, or cases, some of which were described with reference to legal texts, and others as resulting from the need to distinguish itself. From the perspective of *ius*, this made no difference: whether there was a law for resolving a situation or whether it was purely hypothetical, their value for *iurisprudens* was the same. The connection between Right and the reality of the world, be it factual or legislative, was distant and supple; what counted was the way in which this connection could give rise to other connections, within an infinite concatenation of ratiocination. Instead of a system, Gaius's *Institutes* outlined a network – a network based on the unrestricted multiplication of hypotheses connected with each other by virtue of the operation of distinction. This, indeed, was the true nature of *ius*: as an art of operations, it was an art that enabled the unlimited proliferation of hypotheses.

*

§30. Disruption. Where Greek *nomos* developed by equipping itself with the means by which it could separate from the world of *phusis* to better reconcile itself to the order governing it, Roman *ius* saw itself first and foremost as the imagination of other worlds. No order governed this imagination, except for the experimental demand to link up hypothesis with hypothesis, and so operation with operation – this distinction producing that new operation, as was the case with obligation. Learned, casuistic, hypothetic, operational, antagonistic to system and rule, Roman Right was like no other existing legal form – at least for the first four centuries of its development. Because, in the middle of the second century BCE, the transformation of the intellectual structure of Roman society, which had become suddenly fascinated with Hellenistic culture, led to a major disruption in the conception of *ius*. Even while its practice continued to be based on a strict division of labour between those responsible for the administration of justice or legislation and those responsible for juridical invention, its place in the Roman conceptual universe changed. Its status as a logic uninterested in the great questions made fashionable by political thought, starting with the question of justice, began to provoke irritation in the noble souls – an irritation exacerbated by the attitude of the practitioners. Just as jurists in the Athens of Pericles had provoked the ire of philosophers, so the jurists and their esoteric quibbling provoked the ridicule of satirists and moralists in end of the Republic Rome. It had become intolerable to accept that citizens were at the mercy of a pure instrument of thought from which all value, moral, and even reference to humanity, had been evacuated: there

had to be a reason. Since this reason was not to be found in the will of the gods, they too being victims of the kind of necessity deployed by the language of *ius*, it had to be flushed out elsewhere, even higher up. So it was that, after four centuries of innovations, Roman Right was summoned to defend itself before the very category it had obscured: the category of *nomos*.

INTERLUDE 3

§D. *Case.*   Casuistry is the enemy of Law: to give in to casuistic subtleties is to give up on what Law should aspire to, namely the superior dignity of principles, in that they are ultimately what make something like order possible. Unlike principles, cases refuse the distinction between fact and Right; they remain inscribed in the infinite diversity of the diverse, suggesting that it might resist any systemization or logicizing. *The diverse is senseless*: this is the casuistic manifesto *par excellence*; from this perspective, it is impossible to make sense of the world without immediately taking from it what makes the it what it is – namely its tendency to never be what it is. With the casuistic, the ungraspable nature of what *makes* the world is assumed to the point that it is the cases themselves that ultimately articulate its whole as an unbounded collection of always possible new cases. The world flees as world: its being ceaselessly stumbling on the multiplicity of what constitutes it, which, in constituting it, gives the lie to any pretention to unification; the constitution of the world is an inconsistent constitution. It is this fundamental inconsistence of the world that the rule of Law seeks to redeem as it proscribes the casuistic to the benefit of the norm – which is to say: reversing the movement of the juridical such that the world takes second place. With Law, it becomes possible to take precedence over the world – or at least to make out that this is possible, and to draw from this possibility the most radical consequences with respect to guaranteeing order. In truth, this is hardly surprising: since order exists only to the extent that Law can be expressed in it, it goes without saying that Law implies, reciprocally, the possibility of order if it is to be anything more than a pleasantry deserving a mere shrug of the shoulders. Casuistry, on the other hand, has no need to turn to the category of order to pursue its exploration of the world; it needs nothing more than the world; where, from the logical perspective, Law is maximalist, casuistry is minimalist. It has no need for a system of cause or justification to deploy its effects; it requires only the splendid simplicity of what it produces to be considered justified.

4

LEX

§31. Leges. The Romans made very few instances of Law: even at the high point of its popularity, in the centuries immediately preceding Justinian's reign, legislative production in Rome remained negligible. During the millennium from the Roman Kingdom to the proclamation of the *Corpus*, we count only several dozen, at best a few hundred, *leges*, mostly passed during the imperial era. What is more, these laws took forms that would disqualify them from any claim to the title if we were to apply contemporary criteria; the majority were, in fact, simple decisions, even plebiscites. This was especially true of the *leges regiea* or 'royal laws' of the early days, which were more like Greek *thesmoi* than anything else; while laws adopted at the end of the Republic aimed first and foremost at placating the plebeians, who had become dominant. In any case, they had a very different objective from that of *ius*: with just a few exceptions, they were not concerned with questions of private Right, but more with the political difficulties the city was going through. This in no way prevented the Romans from employing a vast range of measures with normative intent that accompanied *ius* like its shadow, without, however, replacing it or, crucially, claiming to cover everything. From their perspective, the *leges* represented a last resort that was only to be turned to when juridical imagination was found wanting – or when a new and urgent question required the attention of the Assemblies or Senate. The fact that they achieved growing success at the end of the Republic and at the beginning of the Empire must, therefore, be understood as a movement towards a different understanding of Right, promoted by some *against* the tradition of *ius*. Where *ius* manifested itself as the theoretical work of specialists who were usually distanced from public life, *lex* was the medium of political debate that enabled its adherents to distinguish themselves in the fundamental disputes of their time. Indeed, the main fault they found with the *iurisprudentes*, beyond the complexity of their reasoning, was that the *ius* whose subtleties they developed looked dangerously like arcana.

*

§32. *Lectio*. The publication of the *Lex Duodecim Tabularum* had settled nothing: the monopoly over knowledge of *ius*, which the pontiffs had enjoyed, had been replaced by another – of specialists even further removed from power, since they were not even nominated by it. On the other hand, the idea of *lex* implied a very different public existence; where *ius* could only be indicated by the *iudex*, Law was made to be read aloud – to be spoken so that it was heard by everyone. If it accompanied the history of *ius*, this was because it came out of an identical ritual context; the type of ritual and the expected effects were, however, different: here it was not a question of efficacy, but of validity. Where in the one instance the delivery of a secret formula meant the necessary setting in motion of forces, the public and solemn reading of a text in the other sought only to assure that it was perceived as the expression of a sovereignty. Reading was a condition of validity, and not an operator of efficacy; it attested to the fact that the source of what was being read was to be found in a legitimate authority – since it was always the responsibility of a magistrate or a priest. Even the ways in which the *iura* and the *leges*, unlike other juridical texts like the *senatus consultum* or the praetorian edicts, both used the imperative mode should be understood differently. On the one hand, it was a matter of creating a constraint from which it was impossible to escape; on the other, of demonstrating the power embodied in the one reading the text – their legitimacy in formulating commandments. The gap between the two was, therefore, considerable, even if it was accepted that *ius* could be produced from a *lex*: for this to happen, however, it was necessary for the law in question to integrate itself into the network of operations defined by the scholars. In itself, a *lex* could only ever formulate an order, a rule or norm, without possessing the means to prevent itself from being ignored by those it addressed – which was not the case with *ius*. If Law was to be anything other than a pure declaration of power, it had to involve the deployment of operations that did not depend on it, but on which it depended: Law was dependent on Right, and not the other way around.

*

§33. Cicero. From the second century onwards, the philhellenism of a section of the intelligentsia led to a reconsideration of this division of tasks, which was thought to result in the worst extremes of injustice and technocracy. The subservience of *lex* to *ius* was what justified the monopoly of the *iurisprudentes* as well as the absurd behaviour of the litigants, always ready, following a cliché as old as Right itself, with the dirtiest tricks. The relationship had, therefore, to be reversed, and *ius* placed under *lex* – which was no longer understood as a simple legislative instrument, but as deploying a general logic, at the heart of which the idea of justice could blossom. Amongst those who championed this reversal most assiduously, and criticized most vigorously the work of the scholars and litigants, we must doubtless include Cicero, who sanctioned many developments. One-time pupil of Quintus Macius Scaevola, the son of Publius Mucius Scaevola, author of the distinction between the real and obligatory effect of agreements, he knew the machinery of 'jurisprudence' very well. The criticisms he dedicated to the sterile, even absurd, character of the scholars' work were most violently expressed in the diatribe of his discourse *Pro Murena*, dedicated to the defence of a young consul accused of corruption. That the accusation had been made by Servius Sulpicius Rufus, a famous *Iurisprudens*, also already cited for his contribution to the history of the concept of obligation, was doubtless a factor in the strategic violence of Cicero's attack. But, ultimately, he was expressing a point of view which for him was fundamental: *ius* had to be stabilized with reference to principles external to it, or the disorder Rome was experiencing would continue. The orator saw these principles working in a kind of *tranlatio imperii*, which

would designate to the masters of these principles the task of directing society's juridical direction – and, through this, its moral and political direction. In short, Right was to cease to be juridical in order that it could be saved from what appeared to be its essential defect.

*

§34. Uinculum. It is in his dialogue *De Legibus*, most likely written over the summer of 52 BCE in the days before his departure for Cilicia, where he had been made proconsul, that Cicero went furthest in his thinking of Right. As the title indicates, this was not a thinking of *ius*; it was a thinking of *lex*, as a general form allowing for the methodical organization of what until then had appeared as formal casuistry. In it, he took up an idea he had already formulated in his discourse *Pro Caecina*, given in 69: that Right constitutes a bond that is not juridical, but linked to communal life and utility (*uincula non modo iudicorum sed etiam utilitatis uitaeque communis*). Where his teachers had sought to think *uinculum iuris* in terms of what would become an obligation, Cicero thought of it as something exceeding all individual relations to encompass the whole of the city. Just as the city could not exist without a governing order, it was necessary that Right accept its own ordering – and that this order develop according to a network of significations that could lend it legitimacy. While he did not hold back in his criticism of Servius Sulpicius, he nonetheless recognized his intention to tidy up the casuistry of Roman *ius*, and that he had introduced into it a classification based explicitly on principles of reason. For his part, Cicero wanted to step up this work by elevating the method Servius Suplicius had elaborated to the level of a true social philosophy built on a finite set of axioms of justice. These axioms, according to Cicero, could only be found in an absolute idea of nature as a fundamental order of the world, within which the totality of principles assuring its proper functioning are expressed. From an improvised art, 'jurisprudence'

was to transform itself into both a rational science and a natural science, built on the knowledge of fundamental rules that would mean it could be considered just. But this could only be done through recourse to *lex*, conceived as analogous to natural law itself – which is to say, the moral legislation bestowing on human beings their place in the world.

*

§35. *Nomos*. In the context of end of the Republic Rome, the appeal to natural reason and to the grandeur of the connection between human beings and the cosmic order could not fail to bring to mind the theories of the Stoics. Cicero, however, emended the Stoicism that was then in fashion by inscribing it in a Platonic intellectual context – where the connection between humanity and nature was synonymous with the movement towards the divine. In order to make amends for the baseness of the operations it authorized amongst the practitioners, Right needed to go back up to the very sources of that which was – sources that only philosophy was able to express. '*Non ergo a praetoris edicto, ut plerique nunc, neque a duodecim tabulis, ut superiores, sed pentus ex intima philosophia hauriendam iuris disciplinam putas,*' he has one of the two interlocutors of *De Legibus* say at the beginning of the dialogue. Meaning: 'It is not, therefore, from the edict of the Praetor, as most do at present, nor from the Twelve Tables, as did the ancients, that the discipline of Right is to be drawn, but from the very heart of philosophy.' For Cicero, therefore, to play *lex* off against *ius*, natural Law against the Right of citizens, was to play philosophy off against jurisprudence – or, in any case, to seek to establish a hierarchy between the two where Right would take second place. The game might have been nothing but a simple appeal to theoretical principle, destined to remain unknown to those it purported to concern; but the rest of *De Legibus* made clear that it was nothing of the kind, and that it was overseen by potent political intent. This intent was the aristocratic restoration of senatorial powers, and the drastic reduction of prerogatives afforded to the people in a whole range of magistracies that, until then, had worked in their favour. The appeal to natural justice and to the supremacy of philosophy over Right barely disguised the ambition to institute in Rome an assertive political and moral order, under the control of the *Optimates* (of which Cicero was one). From the very beginning, the struggle against *ius* took the form of a political combat in which any weapon was admissible, starting with the recollection of the noble origin of *lex*, the source of all things – an origin that Cicero named: '*nomos*'.

*

§36. *Perfectio.* '*Igitur doctissimis uiris proficisci placuit a lege, haud scio an recte, si modo, ut idem definiunt, lex est ratio summa, insita in natura, quae iubet ea quae facienda sunt, prohibetque contraria. Eadem ratio, cum est in hominis mente confirmata et perfecta; lex est. Itaque arbitrantur prudentiam esse legem, cuius ea ius sit, ut recte facere iubeat, uetet delinquere, eamque rem illi Graeco putan nomine* νομου *a suum cuique tribuendo appellatam, ego nostro a legendo*' (VI, 18–19). 'Thus, some of the most learned decided to take law as a point of departure, and rightly so, if, as they define it, it is the supreme reason, embedded in nature, that judges on what must be done, and forbids what must not. This reason, once it is confirmed and established in the minds of men, is the law. They also decided that prudence is law, where rightly it would indicate that the licit be accomplished and the illicit foregone, the very thing to which the Greeks gave the name νομου, in that it gives to each what is their due, and which we have taken from the verb to choose.' For Cicero, things were clear: there was a direct connection between the regime of Law he was calling for and the Greek conception of *nomos*, as an instrument for distributing spaces in a given area. It was this conception that at all costs he wanted to adapt to the Roman world, and language itself was to suffer by it – as we see with the slightly fanciful etymology he suggested for the word *lex*. It had two novel characteristics: on the one hand, it was based on a distinction between the permitted and the prohibited, which was foreign to the culture of *ius*; while, on the other, it emerged as a category of thought that each individual had a duty to integrate. Law, as conceived by Cicero, was not a simple instrument exterior to men, but a way of seeing the world which could only be said to be 'perfect' (*perfecta*) once it was established in the mind of each. This perfection implied, moreover, that the world in question was apportioned such that each received his due – which is to say that every thing was in its place, and that every place received its thing, without any possible argument. And certainly not from the lower classes.

*

§37. *Schola.* The unexpected eruption of *nomos* onto the Roman juridical scene took the form, therefore, of a double power grab: methodological (Law claiming to prevail over Right) and political (the aristocracy seeking to win out over the people). Far from being only the expression of an order transcending the worldly coordinates of public life, it was the emblem of a general policing of institutions and thought, with the declared aim of remodelling them. More than anything, it overturned the meaning of the most basic vocabulary of Roman Right, transferring *lex* to the standing of a regulatory idea, which completely disregarded the technical limits within which it had developed up until then. Even though this gesture produced few consequences with respect to the actual exercise of Right, it had a long-lasting effect on the way in which *ius* was conceived by the *iurisprudentes*, and, most importantly in which it was commandeered by the authorities to serve their purposes. On the one hand, the scholars of the first centuries gave way to the schools (*schola* or *secta*), placed under the authority of figures who had demonstrated the greatest virtuosity and the greatest awareness in the manipulation of *ius*. On the other, their activity now enjoyed a kind of privilege, introduced by Augustus and titled '*ius publice respondendi ex auctoritate principis*', the 'right to respond publicly in the name of the prince'. Since the description of this given by Pomponius in his *Enchiridium* is corrupted, it is impossible to establish the precise scope of this privilege – what must be understood, however, is that the Emperor meant to intervene in the conception of *ius*. This imperial interventionism may not have been what Cicero had in mind when he asserted that it was time for Right to settle under the authority of Law; it no less remains the case that this was a decision that fit with his theory. *Lex* was the Trojan horse (in an almost literal sense) through which the Greek conception of Right as a legitimate civic order was introduced into the Roman world, and ultimately wiped out the creative anarchy of *ius*. In place of an operational casuistry, the Roman juridical model became one based on a system of rules whose objective was no longer to generate, but to authorize or prohibit.

*

§38. *Norm.* Legal positivism did not come into being with *ius*, but with *lex*; it is one of the two faces of a kind of Janus bifrons born of the same conceptual movement, whose other face is the iusnaturalism formalized by Cicero. This movement entails two decisions: the first is the deontic reprogramming of Right; the second is its reinscription in a logic of legitimacy and foundation, which is to say of the *archè* – where *ius* was ontic and anarchic. Until the time of Cicero, Right concerned only being, which its operations might modify at any instant – modifications that were not rooted in an order of causes but in a pragmatics of consequences. With *lex*, this conception found its limit: from an orientation towards the possibilities of being, *ius* was rerouted in the direction of the impossibility of the should; from a tool for exploring hypotheses where only the consequences mattered, it became a barrier. With this change in direction, the aim was to leave the sphere of experimental understanding to enter that of political policing, with those in charge increasingly implicated in the architecture of power. The strange autism of *ius* was to bring about its transplantation into a general ecology of institutions and political forces, within which it could finally play the role that was expected of it, rather than extricating itself from everything. *There could be no Right outside of Law*: this is the maxim that Cicero wanted to see countersigned by *ius*, opening in this way the age of confusion between Right and Law, between the juridical and the legal, between the formal and the normative, which still is ours today. Where, for us, it has become almost naturally invisible, at the end of the Republic this confusion amounted to a theoretical thunderclap – a 180-degree turn with respect to half a millennium of juridical innovations. That it was more or less upheld by a proportion of jurists in the following centuries produced a serious discomfort: the one the educated classes always experience when faced with the spectacle of a world that is not going how they would like. From then on, Right would be inconceivable outside its articulation with a politics and a morality that had become its true masters.

*

§39. *Morality*. The adaptation of the Greek logic of *nomos* to the Roman juridical universe did not only lead, therefore, to the normation of *ius*; it also entailed the moralization of the order for which it served as an instrument. Which is to say, it entailed a kind of principial expropriation of Right from its proper domain – a way of annulling Right by morality, in the very moment that the importance of its normative role was affirmed. Where, in Greece, *nomos* was the simple affirmation of an order to be respected, *lex* claimed to be its active effectuation in the elaboration of the mechanisms that would make it possible – an order where the relation with the divine was no longer one of imitation, but of pretext. For the

Athenians, that the civic order should imitate the divine order was a reflex whose structure was eternal; for the Romans, it was the civic order itself that was rooted in the divine, so far as it yielded to a programme decreed by the interpreters of nature. Which was the reason why, for Cicero as for many of his contemporaries, *lex* was perceived as an instrument of reform: the subordination of *lex* to its requirements would lead to other, more critical changes. Such that, ultimately, it embodied an enigma: on the one hand, it sought to establish clearly the separation of the permitted from the prohibited; on the other, it was expected that it would enable the establishment of new institutions. But it is only an apparent enigma, once it is understood that the creative power of *lex* worked in a radically different way from that of *ius* – the one having the impossible for its operational horizon, and the other the possible. *Lex* culminated in the ineluctable, *ius* made necessary; one implemented a situation within an immutable framework, the other invented new modalities for eluding the framework, when it wasn't reconfiguring the framework itself. Sometimes, in practice, things did not go as expected – but such at least were the basic character-istics of the mode of operation of the two forms of 'Right' that the end of the Republic saw in ruthless confrontation. And if *lex* enjoyed the favour of the aspiring reformers of Roman institutions, it was precisely because it allowed them to lend their initiatives an air of inevitability.

*

§40. *Synthesis*. By the time Justinian set to work on the *Curpus Iuris Civilis*, a long time had passed since *lex* had prevailed over *ius*, and since Right, understood in its broadest sense, had joined the panoply of government instruments. Just a few decades after Cicero wrote his *De Legibus*, Caesar and Pompey had already attempted to draft a great codification, conceived according to the classificatory principles devised by Servius Sulpicius. If it came to nothing, this was doubtless because the reform of institutions that *lex* was to allow was not yet complete – or because the scholars continued to pay it only the minimal attention they reserved for public 'Right'. But five centuries later, the situation had changed to such a degree that even Law had been supplanted by pure imperial decrees: the time was ripe for a synthesis that would be, before it was anything else, a commemorative monument to an extinct art. Unlike Hammurabi's stele, Justinian's *Corpus* was not intended as a demonstration of the moral greatness of a king favoured by the gods; it was a way of fixing for the longest time possible a certain state of the imperial order. That this attempt was a desperate act, and that subsequent events were to prove its failure, is clear from the ensuing history – since codification did not prevent the continuation of imperial interventions. It nonetheless signalled a desire to confine relations between citizens within an increasingly heavy-handed and increasingly restrictive civic constraint – a constraint whereby Law was expected to formulate everything. *Ius*, which had never aimed at everything, but rather at what forever escaped it, could only dissolve in such a programme of imperial policing, born in the dreams of a loquacious philosopher. So, they continued their work without it, nurturing the whole European legal tradition, from the first medieval attempts at codification to the great religious undertakings culminating in 1804 with the adoption of the Napoleonic Code. *Ius* was what the triumph of *lex* excluded – and, with it, the infinite possibilities of invention that *ius*'s mode of operation opened, even if it was *ius* that had provided it with the means.

INTERLUDE 4

§*E. Being.*   There is nothing more pitiful than the division of the world between the 'is' [*être*] (*Sein*) and the 'ought' [*devoir-être*] (*Sollen*), between what is given and what seeks to orient the given according to one of the three modes of deontic logic. The obligatory, the permitted and the prohibited in fact say nothing about the way in which the world itself works; no more than codification is anything but a pure form of the desire to regulate. Orienting yourself in the world with the 'ought' becomes a kind of scholastic exercise, where the only possible operations are respect for the obligatory, or its transgression – with everything that this is assumed to entail. On the one hand, the world as given is delivered in its complete passivity; on the other, acting in it is reduced to the manipulation of certain coordinates in keeping with the deontic demands of some rule, or some applicable norm. From the perspective of the description of what is, as from the perspective of the systems in which human beings act, this is but the sad spectacle of robots moving awkwardly in a theatre of shadows. Beyond this deficiency, however, the distinction between the 'is' and the 'ought' is based, in the first instance, on a selection excluding anything not reducible to one or other of these categories – the very thing that is essential to Right. Right has no interest in 'being' (which it reinvents for fun) or what 'ought to be' (which it knows to be powerless); the only thing that matters to it is what 'may be' [*peut-être*], the possibilities of being, whether with respect to the world, humans, stones or gods. Right is not deontic, it is hypothetic – it is based on an exploratory structure of the world, itself based on the assumption that nothing, or nearly nothing, is known about it, *not least what is thought to be known*. 'Being' is a mystery to it, and it becomes very difficult to maintain that an 'ought' can be imposed when human actions, like those of other creatures, are characterized first and foremost by their unpredictability. Rather than policing surprise, like Law, Right is a means by which to welcome it – a way of providing a place of expression to the permanent surprise at what is and to the bewilderment it is bound to provoke, instead of the pious certitudes of the 'ought'.

5

FIQH

§41. Oumma. Barely eighty years after Justinian decreed his *Corpus* in Byzantium, Mohammed received his first revelation from the mouth of the archangel Gabriel in the cave of Hira on the Jabel al-Nour near Mecca. For the rest of his life, he never stopped preaching the abandonment of polytheism in favour of the unique God, while being forced to flee the persecution of his followers by the powers in Mecca. From the time of his move to Medina in 622, however, his work took a new turn, and became oriented to the establishment of a political and religious community (*oumma*), founded on a principle of general tolerance. This did not prevent the persecution from continuing, in the form of a series of wars and sieges, in which Mohammed would ultimately be victorious, leading to the unification under his control of the various tribes of the Arabian Peninsula. At the time of his death, what had been an unimportant little cult had become the system within which the entire Arab world evolved, governed by the provisions of the 'Constitution of Medina'. Written by Mohammed on his arrival in the town with a view to resolving disputes between several local clans, this text established provisions relating to the coexistence of everyone within the *oumma*. Besides this constitutional settlement, the prophet continued to articulate the grounds of a vague statute that his disciples, thinking it was the actual word of God, noted down. It was these declarations that, once they had been compiled in written form on the orders of the first caliph, Abu Bakr, would ultimately result in the Koran – even though its canon was not established until around 640 during the reign of Uthman, the third caliph. According to tradition, it was at this time that the contents of the Koran were definitively fixed, along with accompanying remarks and stories called 'hadiths', which were attributed to the prophet and considered accessory to the revelation. According to Islamic scholars, these constitute the two primary sources in their study of the divine word, or *sharia* – a study that was known as '*fiqh*', meaning 'comprehension' or 'understanding'.

*

§42. Sharia. The distinction between *sharia* and *fiqh* is essential to an understanding of Islam: where the first designates the totality of the juridical precepts making up the revelation, the second designates the science necessary for their implementation. Without *fiqh*, Mohammed's revelation is destined to remain revelation – which is to say, to remain a simple 'path', open but lacking the equipment needed to follow it. Where *sharia* includes all the rules imposed by God on the believer, such as are found in the Koran or the hadiths, *fiqh* is the tool by which they can be deciphered and, most importantly, interpreted. Even though the word of God must be treated with the greatest reverence, it is not out of the question to sometimes intervene to explain or clarify it, even if only minimally – not to mention to judge its applicability to unexpected situations. This at least was what the first practitioners of the Koran felt when they were attempting to extract the precepts that distinguished it from the juridical provisions still in force from before the revelation. For them, the elliptical nature of the divine word implied the deployment of a set of technical and logical tools without which the uniqueness of Islamic deontology would be unable to assert itself. From the first decades after Mohammed's death, attempts were made that aimed to constitute an effective Muslim Right – attempts that were rejected because of their lack of religious fidelity. When the Umayyad dynasty was overturned by the Abbasid dynasty in 750, these first attempts gave way to a conscious practice of recognizing the role played by learned jurists in the establishment of an Islamic order. It was from this time on that the 'schools' (*madhab*) of juridical thought started to develop their intellectual tools – but also to increase their objections to those who did not think along the same lines as them. This did not, however, stop them from creating two new categories in short order: first, the notion of '*ijma*' or 'consensus'; and, second, that of '*qiyâs*', or 'analogy' – categories completing the range of sources of *fiqh*.

*

§43. Fiqh. When Muhammad al-Shâfî'i published his *Kitab ar-Risāla fī Uṣūl al-Fiqh* ('Epistle on the communication of the foundations of understanding') in 820, *fiqh* was still in a rudimentary state. A quarter of a century earlier, Mâlik ibn-Anas had been the first to attempt to gather the full range of juridical teaching of the first Islamic scholars into a more or less coherent whole, but he had hardly touched the logic. His *Al-Muwatta*, published in 796, was no more than a disorganized compendium of questions, whose main concern was to provide a satisfactory explanation as to the authority of the solution given them. Shâfî'i, however, sought to formulate a list of general principles that would move beyond his predecessors' imprecise reasoning, whatever side they were on, in matters relating to, among other things, revelation. The controversies that shook the Islamic schools during the first two centuries after the death of the prophet were based on the implicit assumption that the community of believers still maintained a direct link with his word. Shâfî'i demonstrated that this was not at all the case: to assert the authority of a solution in the sphere of Right on the basis of revelation implied a judicious reconstruction, in which the respective roles of the Koran, the *sunna*, the *ijma* and the *qiyâs* had to be carefully weighed. If it was self-evident that the revelation had been given once and for all, it was equally self-evident that, as every action of the believer was open to juridical classification, he must have at his disposal the means by which it could be elucidated. From which came the need to provide the *fiqh* with solid 'foundations' (*usûl*), on the basis of which the *faquih* would be free to travel back along the path leading to the source of all truth of all acts, namely the word of God himself. For the Koran, it was a question of returning to the text of the revelation; for the *sunna*, of reconstructing the network of those who had spread the word; and, for the *ijma*, of demonstrating the soundness of the community consensus. The case of *qiyâs*, however, called for special treatment, as it was in the mechanism of interpretation by analogy that the only acceptable possibility for invention could be found.

*

§44. *Qiyâs*. Examining a case using analogical interpretation meant accomplishing something against which the whole emerging edifice of Islamic authority was opposed: the adaptation of revealed law (*ijtihâd*) to situations it had not foreseen. Since it was out of the question that this adaptation take the form of an alteration of the letter of revelation, it was therefore obliged to demonstrate how the novelty had already been anticipated by it – and therefore the fate it had determined for it. Shâfi'i distinguished two different forms of analogy: that based on simple resemblance (*shabah*), and that which could be argued from similar grounds (*ma'na*) – which is to say from a shared explanatory principle. From his point of view, the most important thing was that the use of *qiyâs* excluded all personal assessment (*istihsan*), on the basis that this implied that a human intervention could raise itself to the level of the word of God, which was completely unacceptable. Reasoning by analogy was to become a purely abstract method, an impersonal logical device, whose consequences imposed themselves with the same degree of certitude as if it were guaranteed by a hadith or a surah. Later, the doctrine of *qiyâs* would be refined to the point of the separate theorization of the four terms that made it up (the case, the source, the cause and the statute), but Shâfi'i was happy to assert its principle. For him, it was only important that it could be given an objective definition, such that, regardless of what the followers of other, more traditional, schools would have wished, a place was held open for inventiveness within the structure of Law. If this was not the case, then any attempt to formulate the 'foundations' on which *fiqh* could be based was destined for failure, leaving only a choice between the arbitrary and the most obtuse tradition. To the extent that he rejected the hypothesis that the productions of the first teachers could be integrated into the canon, this implied that Shâfi'i accepted some of the teachings of the traditionalists he criticized. But this was the price to pay if Islam was to be established as a juridical religion whose only authorized interpreters would be the legal scholars – and not the representatives of existing powers, or the judicial authorities.

*

§45. *Shâfi'i.* With Shâfi'i, the apparatus of *fiqh* started to take a particular turn; from now on, the understanding of *sharia* could claim to be based on an original structured set of operational principles. These principles delineated a landscape of knowledge entailing the consideration of 'understanding' as a vital mediation in the relation of the community to Law – but also the acceptance of its unqualified juridical character. Mohammed's revelation was not religious in the sense that it was based on the appearance of a new God; it was the revelation of the conditions necessary for the establishment of relations with a God who had always existed. What the prophet had provided was a rigorous system of connections – a system it was vital not to distort through vague or incomplete relaying, or with unbounded inventiveness. For Shâfi'i, the role of *fiqh* was as guardian of this system: it was the knowledge of connections, and, as such, it was to be implemented through a set of technical categories establishing a discipline extraneous to any political or judicial practice. A crucial epistemological decision attested to the closed nature of *fiqh*: the decision to conceive of its work only from the perspective of substantiation by fidelity to the revelation – which is to say from the perspective of the substantiation of *fiqh* itself. The establishment of the validity of a solution by recourse to *fiqh* was, first and foremost, the establishment of the validity of *fiqh* as such, along with the method and the source that had led to it. Such that, rather than being inscribed in a logic of practical reasoning, based on the immediate needs of a court, it unfolded as an unkempt catalogue of hypotheses, examined as though they had occurred. In fact, whether they concerned real or completely fanciful situations was

of little consequence; the most important thing was that
the hypotheses examined by the scholars thickened the
network of fidelity leading back to the law. To speak of
usûl al-fiqh, as did Shâfi'i (at least according to tradition),
was therefore to speak of a propensity for thought that
continually returned Islam to its foundations, inasmuch as
they were foundations of knowledge.

*

§46. *Furû.* Even if the school associated with Shâfi'i's
name was not the most important of the Sunni schools,
the lesson it offered with respect to the definition of *fiqh*
became Islam's default position on the subject. The thought
that has come down from Malik (Maliki), like that of his
two most important rivals, Ahmed ibn Hanbal (Hanbali)
and Abu Hanifa (Hanafi), accepted its findings without
question, despite their methodological disagreements. In
the centuries following the publication of the *Risala*,
however, the conception of *fiqh* as *usûl al-fiqh* was coupled
with another, not focused this time on the 'foundations',
but on the *furû*, the 'branches' or 'connections', which is
to say, the applications. Since *usûl* could mean 'roots', the
scholarly interest in *furû* completed the arboreal metaphor
and delineated a comprehensive intellectual landscape,
moving between two systems of ramifications. Consistent
with Shâfi'i's doctrine, however, the idea of a *furû al-fiqh*
was only established in the negative form of the set of
constraints it was to respect in order to avoid enabling the
sin of invention. To this end, the method required that the
faquih only be concerned with a hypothesis to the extent
that it allowed him to return to a 'principle' (*als*) from
which the greatest number of possible applications could
subsequently be drawn. The essential tool for this task
was, as Shâfi'i had understood, *qiyâs*, since the regulation
of the operation of comparison it embodied allowed
simultaneously for the greatest possible flexibility and the
greatest possible dogmatism. The recourse to reasoning by
analogy with a view to exploring new hypotheses in fact

established a kind of internal opening in *sharia*, conceived as a space whose closure did not preclude mystery. The fact that the law had been completely revealed once and for all did not mean that its significance was to be measured in just one way, provided the other possible measurements did not call any aspect into question. Nevertheless, the law having been given, a kind of casuistry of novelty became conceivable, where the task was to ensure that the novelty in question appeared as anything but new.

*

§47. *Taqlîd.* At the beginning of the tenth century, a new consensus emerged in the world of *fiqh* which definitively validated Shâfi'i's point of view, while, at the same time, closing the debate on the question of novelty in Islam. Where he had emphasized the importance of subjective 'effort' (*ijtihâd*) on the part of the *faquîh* in the establishment of the foundations of his reasoning, the doctors of Islam decided that the time had come to advance another value. They therefore decreed the 'closure of *ijtihâd*', and its replacement by the idea of 'copy' (*taqlîd*) – no scholar could now claim any title other than *muqallid*, or 'imitator' of those who had preceded him on the path of understanding. From now on, no further debate on the means necessary to establish the sense of the law would be admitted; the only questions open to scrutiny, and the only perspectives to which it would be permissible to refer, were those that had already been cited. According to the principle of *taqlîd*, only schools that had already been identified could be considered resources in the discussion of the content of the law – whether the teaching of a single school was followed, or, on the contrary, incorporated with others. While this decision led to a complete closure of theoretical debate, it certainly did not prevent the proliferation of interpretations on detailed points of Right, whose hypothetic character took a hyperbolic turn. From the moment *fiqh* came to be considered a discipline of pure knowledge, endlessly repeating the grandeur and

the perfection of the law, everything that was had to find
in it an acceptable explanation. Which is why, over the
next thousand years, scholars would, without the slightest
hesitation, debate such apparently bizarre questions as the
conditions of marriage between a believer and a djinn, or
the timing of inheritance proceedings for an individual who
had been turned to stone by a demon. From the perspective
of normal judicial rationality, this was striking proof of
fiqh's fall into the most absurd scholasticism and casuistry
– but this was to forget that *everything*, in *fiqh*, belonged
to the same logic. The absurdity was not a deviation from a
supposedly pure principle; it belonged to the principle itself.

*

§48. Djinn. Juridical knowledge is an absurdity – at
least if it is considered from the perspective of a refusal to
acknowledge that the power of all formalism is to multiply
possibilities rather than reduce them, to authorize rather
than prohibit. The example of *fiqh* demonstrated this
brilliantly: hand in hand with the implementation of its
closure, it developed a capacity to encompass the most
unexpected, surprising and extraordinary phenomena.
The question of marriage to a djinn (*munâkahat al-djinn*)
belonged in this category of insane investigations – but
only if it was forgotten that the technique implemented
to resolve it remained irreproachable. Just as much, at
least, as in the case of an investigation into the rights
of an ascendant over the inheritance of a childless fifth-
degree descendant – a situation it is impossible to imagine
actually arising. And yet, despite its absurdity, it provoked
heated debates that some Imams still conduct today in
the countless juridical forums used by believers to ask
questions online. In fact, the absurdity did not belong to
the hypothesis; it belonged to the mode of reasoning itself,
to *fiqh* as a means of exploring the universe regulated by
God, in which anything might happen. This absurdity
should have been considered a mark of greatness: it was
the best proof that the power of Right is never to give in

to the limits that some believe must be imposed on what is worthy of investigation. Right has no limits other than its ability to deal with what pertains to the unknowable, the impossible or the contradictory; and it is without any ontological ground other than the relations it is able to establish between beings. Even though, in theory, it was limited to relations between believers, in the context of their relation to God, *fiqh*, whether before or after the closure of *ijtihâd*, had no reservations about imagining forms of relations involving djinns or demons. If you think about it, it was no madder than envisaging relations with other, much more mainstream, figures, also rooted in human superstition, like 'property', 'businesses' or 'states'.

*

§49. Tariqâ. The history of the progressive closure of *fiqh* is, therefore, the history of its paradoxical opening to the most unlikely beings and lifeforms – according to a principle of ontological tolerance ordered by *qiyâs*. This principle of tolerance did not, however, extend only to the beings of superstition or belief; it also implicated modes of existence that were the furthest removed from the canon of social life – those, for example, of the *tasawwuf*, or 'mystic'. In a *fatwa* from the early 1370s dealing with the question of the juridical role that a 'spiritual master' (*shaykh*) might play, Ibn Khaldun advanced an unexpected enlargement of the notion of *fiqh*. The role of the *shaykh* being first and foremost to guide his disciple on the 'path' (*tariqâ*) that would allow him to access a privileged experience of the divine, the question arose in Sufi circles as to whether he also possessed a juridical dimension. *Tariqâ*, after all, was a kind of knowledge – and, since all knowledge had its source in revelation, it was appropriate to wonder about the way in which the mystical experience of the path was articulated with the juridical experience of law. In orthodox circles, there was a real fear that this articulation might appear as sudden illumination, an 'unveiling' (*mukâshafa*), exceeding the

bounds of imitation within which knowledge should remain confined. For Ibn Khaldun, the solution was easily summarized: the teachings of the *tariqâ* were to be considered a particular genre of *fiqh* – an 'internal' *fiqh*, a knowledge of the heart, as opposed to the 'external' *fiqh*, a knowledge of the members. Both cases dealt with a form of understanding that was to remain subjected to the demands weighing on the interpretation of the *sharia* in general, and, as a consequence, to the authority of those whose role it was to study it. The *shaykh* was to be considered a *faqîh* who specialized in the knowledge of the heart: while his teaching could explore the ways of devotion and righteousness, it was to stop short of illumination. To make a claim to revelation was to claim to be able to know as much as God, which was unacceptable; this was the only limit to be placed on *fiqh*.

*

§50. *Doubt.* *Fiqh* can know everything, except what God alone can know – meaning that the science of Right is the science of the knowledge of everything, since there is nothing that cannot be said to be juridical. As with Babylonian *dînum* or Roman *ius*, Muslim Right is knowledge before it is norm: it is the assumption of the variety of what is, rather than the regulation of the conduct of what should be. That this knowledge is expressed in an impressive list of permissions and prohibitions is not decisive: these are just the content of the revelation – and not its end, or even its substance. The most important thing, as Ibn Khaldun understood so well, is the way; it is the ensemble of instruments enabling navigation within the normative edifice of *sharia* in order to discern the straightest, most virtuous, path. Such a path has nothing to do with the observance of a structured order, or with the satisfaction brought to the demands of a more-or-less natural principle of justice; it is the permanent questioning of the nature of what is. In other words: *fiqh* is doubt – it is the manifestation of the anguish of one who knows that the manifold will always keep one more surprise, one more unexpected, one more incongruity, in reserve for its student. That the decision should have been taken to constrain the method, and even the possibility of thinking it, far from reducing this anguish, viralized it within the total spectrum of the thinkable. *Fiqh* is the science of Right, in that its duty to know continually reveals itself in ignorance; it is the science of Right not quite knowing if it wants to rise to the level of Law – but knowing that in no circumstances will it ever be able to. Where the defenders of Greek *nomos* or Roman *lex* claimed to be able to exhaust the question of knowledge in the question of duty, the *faqîh* always accepted that duty was nothing without the knowledge that connected it to Law. There is here a remarkable epistemological modesty, together with a total ontological elegance – a modesty and an elegance that accompany casuistry like its shadow, except from the perspective of those for whom only principles matter. Because the only true knowledge is of disorder.

INTERLUDE 5

§F. *Man.* Legalism is humanism: a way of placing the human being in the middle of the world and ordering everything that happens there according to the demands you wish to make of him. In the history of thought, this figure of the human, on which Law purports to impose its deontic regime, more or less corresponds to that of the subject, as inherited from Greek philosophy and the subsequent development of European thought. This subject is a well-known caricature: master of himself, of his thoughts and his movements, endowed with an evident rationality, but who, alas, sometimes sins through deception, and who is destined to work in the service of society and his kind. Right has never needed a human being like this: rather than a metaphysical category, the technical category of 'person' provided it with everything it needed for its exploration of the 'may-be'. Because, if the 'person' is without any quality other than its role as technical marker making possible the deployment of other juridical operations, it can be used to designate just about anything – and not only a human. Here, the 'subject' might be a tree, an animal, a god, an abstraction (like a state or a business), a djinn, and so on, as you will – and, in fact, in the global history of Right, such has often been willed. Because the most important thing is not the 'being' of what is, but the way in which what is fits in the network of hypotheses examining the consequences of some course of action or other, so as to connect them together. To privilege the human subject, on the other hand, implies enclosing the 'may-be' within the finite universe of bodies to be policed, which are made to believe that it is natural for them to benefit from rights or to have to respond to duties. In fact, this is not at all the case, since what is presented as natural is nothing but a logical artifice – just as the category of 'person' is a technical marker, with the advantage that it does not seek to hide it. Where the 'subject of Right' allows for the infinite multiplication of consequences, the 'human subject' defines the limit within which individuals can be confined, as though they were laboratory rats imprisoned in a labyrinth.

6

LI

§51. Confucius. At the time of Confucius's death in 479 BCE, the ideas he had continually espoused throughout his career as an adviser and teacher had not yet permeated Chinese culture in any depth. Instead, they constituted a kind of ambience, a particular atmosphere surrounding a number of traditional concepts that the sage had reinterpreted in his own way, where it was not quite certain what that was. For a clearer understanding, it was necessary to await the progressive compilation of his sayings in the form of a collection known as the *Analects* – a compilation which found its settled form during the Han era, in the second century BCE. Among Confucius' thoughts gathered in the *Analects*, there are many that turn around a strange concept whose history goes back to the origins of China, and which underwent numerous transformations: the concept of '*li*'. A whole chapter of the book is dedicated to it, titled '*li* and music' – although the most significant insights are given elsewhere, some of them coming from disciples of the master, like 'Zhong You'. Among them, we find a distinction outlining schematically the intellectual landscape of the concept of '*li*' through its opposition to the concept of '*fa*', which had also emerged from the depths of time, and was enjoying a resurgence of interest. 'Govern by force of laws, maintain order through punishment (*fa*), and the people will only submit, without feeling the slightest shame. Govern by virtue, harmonize through rites (*li*), and the people will not only know shame, but of its own accord will tend towards the good.' For Confucius it was clear that the heart of any possible conception of order was to be based on the opposition between *li* and *fa*, and the relegation of *fa* to the level of undesirable accessory – a last resort implying failure. If he insisted so much on this notion, it was because it formed the centre of a complete understanding of the world, where 'Right' was one amongst several possible expressions – a 'Right' that revealed itself through 'rite' rather than 'punishment'. Anyone wanting to understand Chinese 'Right' would first have to pay attention to *li* – since the word for 'Right' did not as such exist.

*

§52. *Li.* Confucius supplied no definition of *li*; he was happy to provide an *impression* – an outline, given in the form of questions, anecdotes or ancillary considerations, leaving its signification in the dark. From its etymology, however, we can surmise its sacred, even oracular, origin, the ideogram *li* being composed of the radicals '*shibu*', meaning 'spirit' or 'divinatory altar', and the homophone '*li*', designating an offertory vase. The first meaning of *li* is therefore 'libation', a ritual offering to a divinity or an ancestor – an offering that should be understood to include the act of sacrifice as well as the thing sacrificed, the rite itself as well as the object. Confucius himself acknowledged this: at the time he spoke of it, the practice of *li* implied a whole universe of meaning spanning its appropriation by very different powers, from the Xia period in the nineteenth century BCE to the age of the Eastern Zhou. Particularly during the reign of the Western Zhou dynasty, between the tenth and the seventh centuries BCE, all the ritual gestures enacted by the Chinese population were subjected to a process of institutionalization. Where previously *li* had been practised in religious, social or courtly contexts, they were now instrumentalized by the princes to contribute to the methodical organization of the social system they were in the process of implementing. This social system, which has been saddled with the qualifying adjective 'feudal' by Sinologists, was based on a tight network of relations between individuals, organized according to very sophisticated hierarchical criteria, and expressed in highly visible outward symbols. In addition to their systemization within this relational structure, the Zhou sovereigns sought to separate *li* from their religious sources and to substitute a secular logic, made up of a mix of protocol and etiquette. This included the way in which marriages and funerals were organized, the kind of clothing that everyone was to wear, the speaking order, the way in which to serve tables or greet guests, and so on. From ritual libations, *li* had become the ensemble of gestures through which the relational order was confirmed in every aspect of the social life controlled by the princes.

*

§53. *Relation.* In his remarks, Confucius let it be understood that he did not reject the institutionalization of *li* undertaken by the Western Zhou; on the contrary, his own conception of rites was based on some of its essential features. In particular, he accepted the fact that *li* were to be thought of as a kind of systematic envelopment of relations – a way of ensuring that social relations took precedence over individuals. The most important thing, from the master's perspective, was that rites should *make* society; that there was no society apart from an ensemble of rites through which social relations were crystallized, however hierarchical or unequal they might be. In fact, in his mind, something like a principle of reciprocity regulated the question of hierarchy: whether it was a matter of relations between an ascendant or a descendant, superiors or inferiors, etc., they always went in two directions. Because a *li* always gave form to a relation, providing its effective existence, it never involved just one individual; every relation being rooted in a more-than-one, but never a more-than-two, it always involved two. Without *li*, there is no relation; there is only the set of circumstances according to which two bodies cohabit, attenuation in a pure stochastic of collisions, where it is impossible to establish the slightest consistency. Like the Zhou sovereigns, however, Confucius was seeking to promote a societal consistency, or an idea of society as consistency – as that which rejected the attenuation of stochastics, for which the gimcrack of punishment provided the best example. Thanks to *li*, a consistency could be produced that made any recourse to ideas of punishment or retribution irrelevant – where the very movement of society rendered their intervention useless. In the society of *li*, there was no disobedience, because there was no obedience either; there was only participation in the construction of forms of relation, in that they made action possible. There was no expectation that rites could fulfil a policing function; on the contrary, they made even the very idea of policing, control or judgement absurd, because they gave substance to justice.

*

§54. *Ren*. It is often argued that it was in the nature of *li* to establish a repertoire of gestures and words with an ethical or moral end in view; but, in fact, there was neither ethic nor moral in Confucius: there was only an ensemble of decisions. These decisions related above all to the necessity of respecting the 'five relations' (with the prince, the father, the wife, the brother and the friend), presented as timeless and sacred – when they were in fact instrumental. Similarly, they were inscribed in a larger ecology, where the keystone was the concept of *ren*, of 'human sense', or 'humanity', whose character was written by combining the radicals 'man' and 'two'. Confucius's insistence with respect to *li* was based on his desire to consider that humanity could not exist unless the relations constitutive of the societies in which it was deployed were formalized – which is to say, their formalization produced humanity. *To produce society is to produce humanity*: such was the master's constructivist belief, within which the *li* played the role of operators, and relations the role of structure – once they had been conditioned by rites. If there was an ethic, then it was material through and through: it was embodied in the materiality of the gestures and words that each individual was expected to perform – according to their class and rank. This materialism extended a very long way indeed, since, beyond the public spectacle of ritual, it encompassed the individuals' consciences, bestowing on them their humanity, which had to be convinced that adhering to some *li* or other was good. It was not simply a matter of pronouncing the appropriate words or performing the expected actions; it was also necessary that these be accompanied by a true commitment of the heart, an absolute good faith in their enactment. It should not be concluded from this, however, that ultimately it was a question of the *li* giving rise to a faith; on the contrary, the lesson to be drawn was that conscience itself became material through the rites. Since the ecology of *li* was defined by *ren*, and since only this could render it effective, it had to be concluded that conscience was the gestures, and the heart was the words.

*

§55. *Xing*.   By indexing the concept of '*li*' to the concept of '*ren*', and by opposing it to the concept of '*fa*', Confucius implied without explicitly saying so that rites were foreign to any edict or obligation: they constituted neither laws nor duties. While the Chinese language did not have a word for 'Right', it did have one for 'Law': the word '*xing*', whose semantic register was close to *fa* – which could also sometimes designate Law. The legislative activity to which the Chinese emperors had dedicated themselves since time immemorial was unconcerned with any positive form of 'Right' or even 'justice'; it was, as Confucius said, only a reaction. This was the reaction of a power to a world where order was beginning to falter, and where hearts and consciences were becoming disconnected from the words and gestures constitutive of humanity and society. At just that moment, something inexorable would happen that would entail punitive measures, often of a terrible violence – even if these measures were *never intended to be enacted*. Law, for the Chinese, comprised a text conceived to be useless; it was a simple statement of principle whose aim was to demonstrate the desire of the 'legislator' to play their part in maintaining the course of the world. Which is why the task of proclaiming punishments (laws, in China, were always penal, never civil) should be considered as distinct from that of the formation of rites – a task that was entirely separate. Unlike *xing*, *li* are not proclaimed; they belong to a timeless tradition, where only the details are subject to change; they are without any origin except the spontaneous deployment of the relations themselves. *Rites are natural artifices*; they do not constitute norms formulated in Law promulgated by any power – because, without them, there is no power, any more than there are humanity or relations. Neither prescriptive nor normative, they constitute the pure expression of a 'nature' which is nothing but the movement of what is, whether that involves plants, animals, buildings or men.

*

§*56. Fa.*　　It goes without saying that the history of rites does not come to an end with Confucius; from the Waring States Period onwards, following the death of the sage, their supremacy was contested by adherents of what we know as 'Legalism'. This term should be taken to refer to all those for whom *li* was to be set aside in favour of *fa*, considered the only instrument of power worthy of the attention of a true prince. Where Confucius had sought to think of power and order within a vast apparatus of formalized relations, from which no one, not even the king, could extract themselves, the followers of 'Legalism' continually defended a kind of principle of exception for power. In the most important tracts of the legalist school, like that of Shang Yang, who was chancellor of the Qin State in the middle of the fourth century BCE, Law was presented as a kind of whip designed to subdue the people to the benefit of the prince. Thanks to *fa*, it became possible to instil fear in the minds of the masses, such that they abandoned any vague hope of opposing the will of the holder of power, who was now free to do what he wanted. In other words, *fa* was believed to play the role of wrecker of the order of relations – or, in any case, of an operator cancelling its efficacy within the constitution of society, which could then be restructured. Rather than being a tool for social pacification, Law introduced war into the very interior of human relations, making the prince the only person capable of guaranteeing their efficacy – which in reality was only his caprice. From this point of view,

Shang demonstrated an absolute cynicism: *fa* did not need
to be just, legitimate or justified; it was pure sovereign *fiat*,
from which nothing could be expected except its ability to
reveal the power of the one enacting it. *Fa* deconstituted,
dehumanized and unbound: by promising the worst of
punishments for those who dared an infraction, it was
designed to replace the dense tissue of relations espoused
by Confucius with the arbitrariness of the legislator. As
such, it was not expected to possess any particular quality
beyond its efficacy in serving the politics of the prince.

*

§57. *Shang.* The first chapter of the first book of the
Book of Lord Shang, a tract in dialogue attributed to
Shang, articulates this in no uncertain terms: 'The sage
makes the law, the fool is subjected to it; the first modifies
rites, the second is their slave.' In the rebalancing of
juridical operators that Legalism hoped to achieve, it was
essential that a role be found for *fa* which would allow it
to overshadow *li*, making it just a rule like any other. As
long as rites could still aspire to a formalism without norm,
they remained unassailable; it was therefore necessary to
give them the status of 'Law', just like punishments,
which become *ipso facto* their model. A structure of
formal operations had to be replaced with a structure of
substantial rules, whose control was placed in the hands of
a sovereign authority: the prince. But there was one point
on which Shang agreed with Confucius: the structure
of rules serving as an instrument of government for the
prince was no more considered to take effect through his
will than were rites. On the contrary, the proclamation of
fa participated in a general effort to terrorize the people in
the broadest sense (including, therefore, the noble classes
as well), with the result that punishments never needed
to be exercised. In this respect, the followers of Legalism
shared a general conception of Law with Confucius; in the
same way that the only good law is useless, the only good
punishment glides through the skies without ever touching

down. It must be concluded that, in their conceptions of
the world, Shang and Confucius are very close indeed;
they both thought of 'juridicity' as something destined to
disappear. 'Right' may not have existed in China, but 'Law'
did not have free rein, except to the degree that it absented
itself from the course of the world, where it was just one
factor among others – desired or detested, depending on
the perspective. The desire to punish expressed by the
legalist thinkers was therefore the desire to contribute
positively to the drift of the world in question – where
Confucius could only imagine doing so negatively.

*

§58. *Xun*.   Even though Legalism's teachings enjoyed at
first only a very localized resonance, they sustained subsequent Chinese thought in the manner of a harmonic – with
a different, more sombre atmosphere than Confucian
heaven. The best example of this is probably the *Xunzi*,
the collection of writings by Xun Kuang, a Confucian
philosopher from the end of the Warring States Period
in the third century BCE – the first argued treatise in the
history of Chinese thought. Unlike the *Analectes*, the
Xunzi did no more than assert its reliance on a qualified
anthropology – rather than resorting to the indeter-
minate abstraction of 'nature'. This anthropology, found
in Chapter 23 of the *Writings*, is contained in just a few
words: 'Human nature is bad and what is good in man is
an artifice', says the text's first paragraph. 'Which is why
it is necessary that men be civilized by rules taught by the
masters, and that they be guided by rites and moral sense
so that courtesy and civility come about, as well as culture
and respect for the natural course of things, by which
means order is achieved.' The displacement may have been
subtle, but it was no less massive for that: on the one hand,
order was presented as constructed on the assumption of
the natural course of things; on the other, this construction
was considered anything but natural. The first dimension
was indisputably inherited from the Confucian tradition,

but the second suggested Legalism's voluntarism, using 'rites' in the same way as 'rules' as it sought the correction of man. The magnanimous observation of the naturalness of the 'five relations' had given way to a social *engineering* that, while not displaying Shang's contempt, nonetheless demonstrated a paradoxical relation to the 'nature of things'. Because, if it was a matter of discovering in it the evidence, such that the order so absent in the Warring States Period could finally be attained, this was to be found, in the first instance, in the guise of a distorted humanity in need of correction. For Master Xun, it was in the nature of things to correct the nature of things – and this was the function of *li*.

*

§59. *Form.*   The perversion of *li* in the direction of *fa* quickly became a reality; and yet, the most important thing differentiating it from the Chinese idea of *xing* (not to mention the Western idea of 'Law') remained unaffected by this change. Even as the question of how *li* were to operate was supplanted by the question of their observance, they maintained their resistance to both the edict and the norm; they remained a form without obligation. The *fa* themselves could hardly claim to do more than punish deviant behaviour – and never to incorporate a collection of behavioural parameters demanding conformity into the fabric of the world. To do that, Chinese juridical thought would have had to conceive of subjects whose actions could be referred to abstract rights and obligations – and whose intentional breaches would be liable to sanction. But this did not happen: whether it was a question of *fa* or *li*, they did not relate to subjects, but to indistinct humanity, which was subsequently divided into categories articulated with each other in a complex network of relations. As Léon Vandermeersch has noted, 'juridical formalism' takes place 'after the decision to act is taken, to compel the act to adopt the required form', where ritual formalism 'conditions in advance the modes of action'. From which comes the requirement, in order to establish any norm, of a subject endowed with the ability to decide individually – an ability that rites do not need because decision-taking is delegated in advance to the rite itself. Even when, as Shang desired, 'Right' came down to the will of the prince, as the proliferation of *fa* revealed, they were never expected to actually take place, and no transgressive decision would ever be taken. Just as 'Right' did not exist in China, neither did 'transgression'; there was only the movement of a world order that was either to be followed or adapted to your needs. If there was a scandal, it was not in the possible 'transgression' of a norm; it was located in the very fact of asserting that the nature of things might not be respected.

*

§60. *The pear tree.* The most telling example of this hatred of the violation of the nature of things is found in the collections of decisions consulted by local officials to keep abreast of the rules applicable in their jurisdiction. The *Tang Yin Pi Shih* ('*Cases Decided in the Shade of the Pear Tree*'), particularly, compiled in 1211 by Gui Wanrong, in the reign of the Southern Song, describes many cases demonstrating this directly. These cases, covering a temporal range running from the third century BCE to the year 1000, usually start by relating how the question came to be asked of an accused in the first place. In the minds of Chinese judges, the very fact that they were being forced to consider the applicable *fa* constituted a kind of personal insult, which was expressed in the conviction that any defendant must be guilty – unless it was proved to the contrary. In fact, that you could be accused of anything was already a fault in their eyes – an irreparable tear in the supple fabric of human relations, indicating that it had not been avoided by their simple presence. That someone could be accused of an infraction, without this accusation being absorbed in advance by the ritual play of relations, represented a double failing: the one that was the theme of the accusation, and that of the judge himself, who had failed in his task. *To accuse someone of a crime was to accuse the judge himself*: this was the reasoning behind the extreme severity of the interrogation procedures to which the accused was subjected – or the punishment risked by the accusers if they had moved too quickly. Like punishments and laws, good judges were useless judges – those whose wisdom forestalled conflicts before they could arise, so the questioning of the ritual order of relations never took place. Flicking through the pages of the manuals of jurisprudence, this is what the judges would learn before anything else: they would not learn to judge, but *to not judge* – to ensure that the circumstances prevented them from doing so. Rather than a prized possession, 'Right' was an indelible mark on the face of humanity, which was to be covered as best you could – or which you pretended not to see.

INTERLUDE 6

§G. *Sanction.* Of all Law's attributes, the most useless is doubtless the sanction; and yet, it is the one that has, from the beginning, aroused most interest among the champions of Law – as though it were here that its essence could be found. Without sanction, there is no Law; there is only an utterance with normative ambition, whose generality and abstraction awkwardly hide its total absence of authority beyond pure intimidation. But what is a sanction? According to the definition accepted in the West, it is the punishment awaiting someone who is reckless, ignorant or daft enough to dare transgress the prescription contained in a law that is recognized as such. The sanction is the means by which Law provides for its own inefficacy – and by which it makes anyone who reminds it of its impudence pay, according to a strange principle of retribution, like that of a capricious or jealous child. In fact, what Law sanctions is not so much the non-adherence to its principle: it is rather the reminder of its inability to ensure that its observance is guaranteed – its inability to fulfil its function. *Law is impotence*: it is living testimony to the fact that it is not the sanction that constitutes its essence, but its transgression – because this is what renders it Law, which is why it is obliged to anticipate it. In other words: *Law exists only in its transgression* – only in the reversal of its functioning, of its invagination in what is supposed just to be an exception, which becomes, as a result, the one true Law. So, we understand that Law needs its vengeance – because what could tolerate existing only as the absolute opposite of what it claims to be, as the pure negation of itself, except nothing? We must, therefore, conclude: from the perspective of the logic of the sanction, Law is nothing; it is a void resting on the possibility of being fulfilled by a transgression finally giving it the possibility of proving its worth. That this worth boils down to the policeman's baton or the orders of the prince is just the way things are: in the same way that the site of power is empty, the instrument it uses in its effort to close the breach must be so as well.

7

GIRI

§61. Ritsuryô. The influence of Confucian juridicity made itself felt far beyond China; in Japan, for example, it very soon came to guide the adoption of a series of legislative provisions inspired by traditional Chinese codifications. The first of these was the edict of Taishi Shôtoku (appointed regent of the Empire at the beginning of Empress Suiko's reign) promulgated in 604 and inaugurating radical reform in the country. This edict, which was followed in 645 by the Taika Reform ordered by Kôtoku and then, in 701, by the Taihô Code requested by Emperor Monmu, is one of the most important texts of the reform movement known as '*ritsuryô*'. The word, which referred to a body of rules, was composed of two concepts, emphasizing its essential division: '*ritsu*', meaning 'punishment', and '*ryô*' meaning 'council' – so, in short, 'criminal code' and 'administrative code'. For Prince Shôtoku, and those who came after him, it was important that the empire over which the Asuka dynasty reigned should be governed in such a way that Japan ceased to be a fragmented country open to potential invaders. On the administrative side, therefore, the *ritsuryô* edicts worked towards the constitution of a hierarchical apparatus of civil servants, distributed over a territory divided into 'provinces' (*kuni*), 'districts' (*kori*) and 'villages' (*ri*). As well as a new territorial division, this distribution implied the emancipation of the peasants, who were placed under the control of the imperial power as the only possible source of authority – which did not fail to provoke resistance from the barons. Similarly, on the penal side, the reforms sought to establish a single punitive system, reserving the devolution of the power to punish for the imperial authorities, to which the local nobles and civil servants were to be subordinate. For Prince Shôtoku, this maximal centralization of power was a necessary condition to obtaining the political effects he was pursuing – effects that were nonetheless presented in moral form in the different edicts. Because the inspiration behind the prince's reforms was in fact none other than the Tang Code, decreed in 624 by Tang Goazu, the first emperor of the dynasty.

*

§62. *Tang.* In Chinese juridical history, the Tang Code was not the first compilation of *fa* ever to be attempted; it was, on the contrary, something of a habit, going back to the mythical kings of the Xia dynasty, like Yu the Great. The undertaking of emperor Goazu was different from those of his predecessors, however, in the scope and systemization of its organization, involving twelve distinct sections and gathering five hundred articles. The emperor's objective was to achieve, by reformulating the punishment regime weighing on his subjects, regardless of their rank, the pacification of the social world, the chaos of which was behind his ascent to the throne. The Tang Code was meant to exert a calming influence on the population – at the same time arranging without delay the concentration of power in the hands of the emperor, in a Legalist mode. In fact, the articles of the Code happily mixed Confucian and Legalist ideas in a way that recalled, in its meticulous desire for control, the pessimistic tones of Master Xun's discourse. Once again, however, the most important thing remained the idea of relation, which governed the collection of provisions gathered in the compilation and was a decisive factor in countless cases. But, contrary to the view of Confucius and his disciples, this factor was motivated more by the need to keep account of positions than by the formation of a humanity conceived as an ontological virtue. The nature and direction of the relation (from ascendant to descendant, for example) served as mitigating or aggravating circumstances within a punishment economy that had chosen to concentrate on details rather than principles. It was this fastidiousness in the harmonizing of the administration of punishment with the social structure of relations that served as an example for Prince Shôtoku in the definition of the juridical apparatus that was to structure the Japanese empire. His edict and those that followed all worked towards the elaboration of a casuistic complex of relations, whose two slopes were the penal code and the administrative code – to the exclusion of any civil code, or any procedure.

Ritsuryô was not so much a reform of Right as a reform of governance.

*

§63. Shôtoku. Even though it resulted in a great many practical changes, this reform never appeared as a legal text or a constitution; instead, it took the form of a kind of credo. The seventeen articles of the Shôtoku edict formed no 'rule', nor even a 'directive'; they did no more than present an improved vision of the world, determining everyone's respective position. The first article outlines the horizon of this vision of the world: 'Harmony is to be valued and the avoidance of conflicts honoured. All are affected by bias, and there are few human beings who can see far. Hence, they disobey their lords and fathers, and harbour feuds with their neighbours. But when the higher ranks are harmonious, and the lower friendly, then calm prevails in the discussion of business, and the correct perspective gains acceptance.' From the first words of the article, the Confucian references are crystal clear: the pursuit of harmony recalls the concept of '*yi*' in Confucius, while its anthropological pessimism is reminiscent of the *Xunzi*. Most tellingly, the definition of society in terms of vertical and horizontal relations, to be activated so they can be productive and allow for the avoidance of any conflict, constitutes the core of Chinese juridical logic. It was this logic that the prince hoped to introduce into the Empire, establishing it through the ensemble of penal and administrative reforms that were enacted alongside. As such, however, the latter were badly received; they failed as soon as they were enacted, the noble clans having no intention of allowing the empress and her regent to gain the upper hand. Yet, the spirit of the edict was to endure; through it, an indigenous version of Confucianism was established on a sustainable basis, accepting its essential premises but rejecting those that were inimical to Japanese ideas. This is how we should understand the grounding of the emperors' power in a genealogy going back to the goddess

Amaterasu, the *kami* of the sun, where Confucianism considered the prince to be the 'son of Heaven' – an emanation of the nature of things.

*

§64. Horitsu. The juridical history of Japan opened, therefore, on a paradox: on the one hand, Prince Shôtoku hoped to acclimatize juridical Confucianism to the Japanese situation; while, on the other, this acclimatization failed to reform its political structure. Even though they were omitted from the edict, it was in the realm of personal relations that it was to have its most significant success, since Japan, like China, developed a profound distaste for any form of juridical intervention in the entanglement of human connections. These relations, which gave structure to the community, were to be cultivated rather than regulated – a culture not of imposed norms, but of mutual obligations seeking to avoid any form of conflict. As in China, this rejection of normativity emerged from an absence: the fact that the Japanese language, just like the Chinese, had no word for 'Right', in either an objective or a subjective sense. The only word, in Japanese, designating something like a rule is the word '*horitsu*', whose original Chinese graphic form, *ho*, indicated the element of water, an imaginary animal able to distinguish the just from the unjust, and the action of disappearing. *Horitsu* is the means by which the just order is re-established, such that, like tranquil water, nothing should trouble its fragile surface – an order that, in its Japanese conception, belonged to the noble classes. 'Law', in Japan, was therefore a means of ensuring that the nobility was not disturbed – a translation of the Legalist logic of punishment, with the added benefit that it did not seek to disguise itself in the trappings of generosity. In contrast to this idea of the rule as pure punishment at the service of those maintaining order, however, the Japanese made use of another concept to account for the logic of relations – a concept foreign to the universe of rules. This was the concept of '*giri*', expressing

the idea of 'good behaviour' – '*gi*' meaning 'just, correct', and '*ri*' meaning 'reason, reasonable behaviour'. *Giri* designated everything that made an individual behave in a way that was acceptable with respect to others, according to their social status – which might include obligations and duties as well as emotions.

*

§65. *Giri*.   To the casual observer, *giri* is always liable to be confused with *li* from the Chinese tradition; in fact, they are very different concepts, reflecting distinctive decisions taken by the two worlds. Where, in the Chinese context, rites are instrumental for relations whose structure they help to constitute, to the point of being inseparable from it, *giri* is neither accessory to nor structural in the system of relations of Japanese society. It constitutes, rather, its *atmosphere* – the emotional tone of its extension, as it embraces the totality of subjects implicated in it, whose only means of extracting themselves is exile. To enter into Japanese society is to enter into a system of perceptions and emotions where any relation finds itself affected by inevitable variables so acute that they come to question even this inevitability itself. There are several orders of variables, but they all involve at least the following aspects: the sense of duty, the absence of force, temporal duration, the expression of affection, the idea of hierarchy and the absence of constraint. Meaning that *giri* is primarily a sensation of duty, whose fulfilment can be demanded by no one, and is therefore endless; it conveys a form of empathy to otherness; it is expressed differently according to the position occupied in society; and, most importantly, it can never be subject to imposition from the outside. Neither social norm, nor formal ritual, nor traditional custom, nor property of humanity, it represents a kind of affective resource, simultaneously vague and very precise, without which there is no possible relation – or at least no substantial relation. With *giri*, the way in which 'Rights' and 'duties' circulate becomes a pleasure or a discomfort; the obligatory relation is not here 'rational', but passionate, as a higher form of the rational. To verify this, one need only consider the only conceivable sanction: shame – while the highest value in play here, named '*ninjō*', is nothing but the 'natural human affection' that each owes to the other. For the Japanese, it is the nature of things itself that is affective.

*

§66. *Emotion.*   It would be a mistake, therefore, to think of *giri* as defining some kind of moral norm, on whatever basis; rather than a rule of a moral nature, we should see here a sensitive mode of perception of relations. In other words: *giri* would be the mode by which the Japanese feel their relations to others (relatives, colleagues, friends, etc.), deducing the gestures, words or actions that their perception induces. That these affective perceptions are encoded in one way or another is not in doubt; but it would be wrong to conclude from this that they orient behaviour, or even that they are themselves oriented. It is characteristic of *giri* that it has no right to require a particular application; it simply appears, without this appearance producing any effect besides a change in emotional register in the relation. To be in a relation of *giri* with someone is *displeasing*, and this displeasure constitutes everything about it – its nature, operator or effect – without any of these being in a position to determine the consequences. Compared with *li* or even *fa*, whose only affect is fear, *giri* therefore introduces a much broader range of affects, which, importantly, it integrates into the logic of relations, rather than seeing them as just ruses to be activated. Even filial devotion, considered by Confucius the model for all forms of relation, only entailed, despite the requirement of its deep integration in the soul, a kind of reverential fear in individual minds. With *giri*, besides the fact that the parent/child relationship is just one of many instances within a network of relations, it does not produce a kind of quasi-mystical paralysis, but a warmth.

The *giri* of the child with respect to its parents, if properly accomplished, is the means by which the family is formed as a haven of peace, a source of feelings of security and intimacy; without it, it is nothing but a cold encounter between separate beings. So, it is understandable that legal mechanism should still today be rejected by the Japanese: it will never replace the emotions of *giri*.

*

§67. *On.*   When she published *The Chrysanthemum and the Sword*, the book that came out of the report she was commissioned to write by the Office of War Information during the Second World War, Ruth Benedict made a crucial mistake. Her mistake was to index the functioning of *giri* to that of a system of debts that the Japanese were intimately obliged to settle – the heaviest of which being *on*, the 'burden' to be borne as best you could. According to Benedict, 'virtue' in Japan was to be defined in terms of the response of each individual to the different *on*, through which they found themselves indebted to their parents, teachers and superiors, going all the way up to the emperor himself. It was the existence of this aggregation of duties that categorized Japan as a country based on a 'shame culture', whereas others, like America, were based more on a 'guilt culture'. Faced with such shame, *giri* constituted a possible means of settling the debt, a technique that would enable the individual to relieve the burden weighing on their shoulders – a settling that Benedict characterized as 'mathematical', which is to say even-handed. Besides this equitable repayment, there was, she added, another form, where, due to an exorbitant aspect, the obligation could never be completely repaid: *gimu*. In both cases, the most important thing was that the repayment procedure was secondary; *on* was primary, and any action undertaken by an individual was undertaken in its disturbing presence. But Benedict was wrong: from the existence of *on*, it does not follow that *giri* should be subordinate, or that it is only a cunning attempt to offload

the burden in order to live a lighter life. *Giri* is not about
offloading anything; its nature is rather to circulate within
relations like blood in the veins; more than a strategy
for avoiding shame, it constitutes its sensible experience.
To distinguish between obligation, shame, and *giri*, and
articulate them with one another as though they formed a
logical construct, is to exclude the thought that it is, before
anything else, a way of being.

*

§68. *Assessment.* *To be is to be affected*: such is the
maxim governing the operation of *giri* – or, rather, that
defines its singular necessity with respect to the demands
of Law and morality, which are unbothered by it. There is
no relation that is not entirely *moulded*, from the perspectives of both form and matter, in an affect, which also
determines its direction – including the relation of 'duty'.
The consequences are clear: duty is also an emotion; it is
not a mechanism rooted in a dimension other than being;
on the contrary, it is completely conflated with it, in that
it is nothing but relations. *Giri* is an ontological apparatus
of juridicity – a way of producing necessity from the
core of what is, or the way in which that which is can
be deployed in the world in a mode that always exceeds
it. If being is being affected, it means that being is a
supplement to itself – that it is nothing but the aggregate of
directions determined by the network of affections, never
in need of a norm, a rule or even an obligation. When
Benedict considered *on* as an obligation, she was wrong:
it is not a normative moral category, but an emotional
ontological category – a category contributing to setting
being in motion. The ought of morality or legality (which
is ultimately the same thing) is completely foreign to it; in
relations between human beings, there is no valid deontic
operation: there is only navigation on the sea of affects.
Which is why the seventeen articles of Prince Shôtoku's
edict, which were still considered to be in force until the
Meiji constitution was adopted in 1989, were formulated

in such a predictable way. No commandment was decreed in it; all that could be read there were general assessments relating to the role that everyone was supposed to occupy within the imperial edifice – without that supposition turning into a duty. *That was how things were* – even if the fact that things were that way did not mean it was impossible that elsewhere, in another context, things might work differently, implying another relational cartography.

*

§69. *Kyaku.* Even if Prince Shôtoku's edict had lent a touch of Confucian dignity to something that, from the perspective of private relations, did not really need it, its high level of abstraction required, on the penal and administrative side, some clarifications. The Taika reform and the Taihō code provided many of these – but it was mainly through 'decrees' that the imperial court sought to compel local *seigneurs* to apply the new rules they had proclaimed. These 'decrees' (*kyaku*), along with 'regulations' (*shiki*), constituted the two main normative instruments available to civil servants and court ministers, who used them massively in the two centuries following the *ritsuryô*. They were compiled and put into order in the eleventh century by an anonymous specialist in Right under the title *Ruijû sandai kyaku*, 'Collection of Decrees from Three Eras' – namely the Kônin, Jôgan and Engi eras, running until the year 907. The decrees covered all spheres of local authority activity, from armament to bridge maintenance, from public stores to rice calibration, from taxes to regulations concerning how the emperor's birthday should be celebrated. We should not, however, be deceived by their fastidiousness: while they expressed the will of the court minsters, their meticulousness above all testified to the difficulties encountered in the enactment of the *ritsuryô* reforms. The decrees were the best proof that they were only followed with difficulty – and still today historians wonder whether, despite the threats of punishment at the end of certain *kyaku*, these latter were ever implemented. The *Ruijû sandai kyaku* nonetheless indicate the extent to which, despite the will of the imperial authorities, the administrative and penal spheres baulked at being incorporated into a system that dreamed of normativity. Something like a kind of *giri* also operated in the public sphere, which, while doubtless based on opportunism and the local conservation of power and wealth, for all that still existed. Claiming to intervene directly in his subordinates' business, the emperor actually introduced more disorder than anything else.

*

§70. Rei. Such was the basis of the Japanese conception of 'Right', a basis it shared with the Confucian conception: *Law brings disorder* – it is what introduces insecurity where security prevailed. Rather than being a constructive tool, Law is a destructive tool, whose principal mode of operation is the cold violence it generates within the subtle network of affects circulating amongst individuals. Of course, it is perfectly acceptable to consider that this is precisely where it is useful: at times when *giri* prevents any possible innovation, reform by Law makes society's reanimation conceivable. At a time when Confucianism had overcome any other vision of the world, during the Tokugawa period in the seventeenth century, the scrupulous observation of *li* (*rei* in Japanese) produced a kind of total social immobility, which there was no hope of shifting. Every word and every gesture found itself bogged down in rites that it was unthinkable to challenge, and whose semiotic had for its sole aim to signify again and always the same order. Yet, this was a misunderstanding: the victory of *li* was actually the victory of a distorted form of Confucianism, which, under Legalism's influence, had forgotten that rites only make sense to the extent that they *produce* relations. This is what *giri* continued to embody, *against* the deathly rigidity of the juridical life of the administration and aristocracy – a supple machinery of affections, open to all transformations. There was no

need, where private relations were concerned, to introduce Law: on the contrary, every time a legislator intervened, the change made life more complicated, more impossible even, on at least one point. This is how, for example, the prohibition on the mixing of sexes in public baths, the *sentō*, was first decided in the Tokugawa era; then, when it was lifted, a shocked Commodore Andrew Perry demanded that it be reinstated. As soon as the representative of Western Law encountered the ritual concerns of the followers of the rite, what until then had not posed a problem for anyone started to create difficulties – and Law was the instrument of choice for this new policing.

INTERLUDE 7

§H. Reason. The equation balancing Law and reason belongs to the original structure of *nomos* – to its Aristotelian interpretation at least, which came to define Law as reason with passion removed. It is an equation harbouring many surprising corollaries, the first being that if reason needs to be separated from passion, this is doubtless because it was formerly possible to confuse them. *There is passion in reason* – and it is this passion that must be cleared out if you are to arrive at Law; as such, however, reason has no licence to deprive itself of its passionate dimension. A second corollary would have Law embody this pure form of reason – Law would be embodied reason, meaning it would be what reason pursues as it works to purify itself of what affects it. *Law is reason's ultimate goal*: there is no pure reason without Law, defining not the content but the form itself – its completion in the perfection of an ordered functioning, homogenous with the order of the world. In other words: there is no reason except of order, and there is no order that is not reasoned – and therefore traversed through and through by the form of rationality that is Law, itself conceived as rational through and through. Because Law cannot be the ultimate goal of reason unless it is itself rational, unless passion plays no role in it, it being understood that passion leads to disorder, and *who knows where* disorder leads. This is essentially the interest of the equation of Law and reason: to put the finishing touches on the edifice authorizing the exclusion of what is not known, which, because it is not known, it is not wanted that it be known. The inscription of Law in the ecology of reason (and vice versa) is the inscription of order in the ecology of intentional ignorance, of the wilful self-prohibition of discovery or surprise. Reason, in Law, has no other role to play: it is there to ensure that nothing happens that has not already happened and will carry on happening for as long as possible – as useless, moronic, futile and bereft of interest as it might be.

8

DHARMA

§71. Smriti. When the most important *Dharmasutra* came to be compiled, certainly between the middle of the third century and the end of the first century BCE, it had been a long time since the revelation received by the sages of ancient times, the *rishi*, had come to an end. The era of *shruti*, of 'hearing', had given way to the era of *smriti*, of 'memory', of the recollection of the divine words transcribed in the *Upanishad* and the *Vedas*, and the exploration of the traces left by them in consciousness. In truth, these traces were overlaid by a great many practices, rituals, taboos, habits, traditions and rules that made the Hindu juridical world an infinitely layered space. The only thing that helped bring unity to this stratification was its structuration by a singular principle, traversing all dimensions: the principle of *dharma* – which the *Dharmasutra* were there to elucidate. The word '*dharma*', derived from the Indo-European root *dhr–*, signifying the action of keeping, maintaining or supporting, means, according to the definition provided by Robert Lingat, 'that which is firm and durable ... that which prevents fall and disappearance'. In ancient Hinduism, *dharma* is, therefore, the constituting principle of that which is, inasmuch as this principle works towards its perpetuation – inasmuch as it is what prevents its destruction or collapse. In other words, it is the response to a threat: the one that forever weighs on the whole world, always in danger of disappearing if it is not cultivated in such a way that hostile forces are kept at bay. It was to the study of this culture that the precepts articulated in *Dharmasutra* were devoted, which were to be read as so many *formulas* enabling everyone to contribute to the survival of the world. These formulas took the form of recommendations covering seemingly completely heterogenous subjects, from the logic of study to the preparation of food, from how baths should be used to rules regarding marriage rites. Superficially, they could be confused with 'Laws', if the very ideas of 'Law' or 'Right' were not completely foreign to Hindu knowledge; rather than 'Right', it was a question of *smriti*, or knowledge.

*

§72. *Sutra.* The *Dharmasutra* were the *sutra* of *dharma*;
they followed the 'thread' (*sutra*) of *dharma* by revealing,
in the form of aphorisms, what it entailed in a whole
series of spheres constitutive of the order of the world.
This thread, however, could not be followed by everyone
– or rather, while it could be followed by everyone, the
knowledge it promoted was oriented favourably towards
a particular 'class' of individuals: the Brahmin. Indeed,
every *sutra* began by explaining that the world was
divided into four 'classes' or 'castes' (*varna*), so, besides
the Brahmins, there were the *Ksatriya* (warriors), the
Vaishyas (merchants) and the *Shudras* (servants). If the
Brahmins, the 'priests', were the main recipients of the
message of the *sutra*, it was because only they dedicated
their lives to studying the *dharma* – but they did not in fact
hold a monopoly in this. Anyone, provided they accepted
the need to behave as an *arya*, as an individual who, in
their conduct, worked for the culture of the world, was
entitled to devote themselves to study, which is to say to
the deepening of understanding through the practice of
precepts. Understanding, in the logic of the *dharma*, was
not learning; it was to act in conformity with the stipula-
tions of the *sutra*, since it was from this conformity that
the *dharma* itself was strengthened; to understand was to
do. This implied that the *dharma* contained much more
than a simple general principle; the order of the world, if
it was to persist, was embodied in the first instance in the
multiplicity of actions, gestures and rituals, etc. involved
in its study. The first and oldest of these were the gestures
of 'sacrifice' (*yajna*) – the means by which, thanks to the
meticulous repetition of a ritual, the world is sewn back
together, re-established in its threatened continuity. To
perform a sacrifice was equivalent to studying, since the
procedure to be followed when carrying it out was based
on recollection, the activation of an ancient knowledge,
whose source was to be found in the accounts of the first
revelations. The word '*dharma*' must therefore be understood in at least two ways: as indicating the consistency of

the world; and as signifying the ensemble of practices on which this consistency was based.

*

§73. *Trivarga.* The *dharma* was not, however, the only source of precepts to turn to if you were uncertain as to how to behave; there were two others besides, whose status was more ambiguous: the *kama* ('pleasure') and the *artha* ('possession'). Just as there were *Dharmasutra*, there were also, therefore, *Kamasutra* and *Arthasutra*: 'threads' by which pleasure and profession, just like study, could contribute to the weaving of the world. Since, however, *dharma*, *kama* and *artha* arranged themselves to form what Hindus call *trivarga*, or the triple path to 'deliverance', *moksa*, it must be surmised that they all share a number of characteristics. Pleasure and material wealth might therefore start to look like study, while *dharma* could just as well unfold within *kama* or *artha*: pleasure and possession could also represent forms of knowledge. Which is why, contrary to a common misconception, the 'aphorisms of pleasure' making up the *Kamasutra* do not constitute a manual for the exploration of arcana, but a means by which to be delivered of them. The most important thing was that the one on the path to deliverance, and so to the strengthening of the consistency of the world, found his own balance between the three aspects of the *trivarga* – this balance being also *dharma*. This means that, in classical Indian thought, *dharma* is not only cosmic or ritual, it is also individual; *dharma* is not general, it unfolds singularly following the 'threads' of each existence. Not only does each *varna* respond to differentiated demands in contributing to the stability of the world, but this takes place always as a specific amalgam of study, pleasure and work. Which also explains why the Brahmin are not the only ones to receive the deliverance that comes from respect for *dharma*: study is everywhere in *dharma*, but it is not everything. Similarly, this explains why being Brahmin is not incompatible with a worldly

existence answering to the concerns of the other classes –
with the exception, that is, of the *Shudra*.

*

§74. *Pramana.*   To open the *Dharmasutra* was, therefore,
to appreciate that not everything was contained within; it
was also to appreciate that the *sutra* themselves stressed
this right from the start, by way of an aphorism on the
sources of the *dharma*. The two Books of *Dharmasutra*
in the Kalpa Sutra of Apastamba, a Vedic master active
somewhere between the ninth and the thirteenth century
BCE, provide a remarkable example of this. 'And now, we
are going to explain the *dharma* accepted by tradition,
whose authority ('*pramana*') is based on the acceptance
of those who know it, and on the *veda*', says the first
aphorism of the first book. Its meaning is clear: the
dharma has three possible sources, namely tradition (as
corroborated by the masters who study it), the texts
of the *veda*, and the *dharma* itself – the *Dharmasutra*
defining the list of sources as such. Reading an article like
this, it is very tempting to conclude that the question of
the *Dharma* can be settled through a direct comparison
with 'custom', as it is understood when we speak of
vernacular forms of right. Ultimately, the juridicity of
dharma would be the juridicity of usage accepted by
recognized authorities, the main characteristic of which
would be their implementation over a long period within
the practices of a given community. But this is not at all
the case: when the *Dharmasutra* speak of tradition, they
do so to insist on the kind of authority that is peculiar to
them, which is summarized in the word '*pramana*', 'valid
knowledge'. If a certain kind of practice is acknowledged
to embody *dharma*, this is because it produces knowledge
that contributes to individual deliverance and the solidity
of the world; it is not because it is just – or even legitimate.
In Hinduism, it is never a question of the good, but of the
true; the authority of a tradition is not of a moral, political
or juridical nature, but *epistemological* – it refers to the

possible means of knowledge. The sources of *dharma* are therefore the knowledge of knowledge, the knowledge of the *veda* and the knowledge of the *dharma* – meaning the knowledge of the one who knows already.

*

§75. Arya. All *dharma* is contained in the individual: it is through his actions that the destiny of the world is played out – and it is through his actions that he might discover the knowledge that will allow him to work for its survival. The order of the world is not something to be conformed to; it results from the study practices of those concerned with the possibility of its continuation; *dharma* is the product of the *Arya* and not the other way around. The *Arya* are, however, expected to study the *kharma*, and draw from this study a stimulus to their behaviour – even, when this behaviour is inappropriate, submitting to sometimes quite severe sanctions (*danda*, or the 'stick'). Here again, the *Dharmasutra* make a fundamental distinction between those engaged in study (like the Brahmins, or the *Ksatrya* who are instructed according to the *veda*) and those who only act in accordance with it. The first book of Apastamba's *sutra* expressed this distinction when it set the punishment for murdering an individual as equivalent to the value of a quantity of cows, while that of a student resulted in voluntary exile. The person responsible for the death of a Brahmin was to build themselves a hut far from any town, keep a careful eye on their language, carry a skull and a banner with them, dress completely in rags and practise begging. After twelve years of asking for their daily bread, declaring themselves a 'hideous sinner' and stepping aside to let anyone they came across pass them on the road, they were considered purified and restored to their previous standing. The fact that this punishment was voluntary was a decisive aspect of the process of purification: the game was not being played at the level of social equilibrium, but at that of individual fate. To commit a sin was to tarnish

your *karma*, and so to threaten the possibility of deliverance as well as the structure of the world – or, better, the possibility of deliverance *as* structure of the world. Indeed, since *dharma* encompassed any action connecting the subject to the cosmic order, we should conclude that *dharma* is *karma*, and vice versa; the fate of an individual is the fate of the whole cosmos.

*

§76. *Abjection.* For Hindu thought, the 'stick' is therefore an integral part of study; it is the means by which each individual trains for their deliverance as they test out the conditions of their admission. Punishment is not retribution in the sense that it would represent a kind of reparation demanded by society from those who have broken its rules; it is the condition of possibility for the perfection of everything. When the world is threatened, this threat can only be averted if mistakes are rectified; but, in order to be rectified, they must have been committed – as they are by every student. The error is not *bad*, just as the one who commits it does not become criminal as a result; rather, it is a question of a stain that needs cleaning, of an obstacle on the road which, because it implicates each and every action, is beyond measure. Once again, the *dharma* is no more moral than it is legal: it is epistemological and cosmological – it involves the possibility of knowledge inasmuch as this is the form taken by the saving of the order of things. Which means that no one finds themselves *subjected* to a punishment, even if it has been decreed by a king; rather than be subjected to a sanction, the individual is enveloped, filled or saturated by it: he himself *becomes* the sanction. Which means that there is no subject in Hindu juridical thought; there are only what we might call *abjects*, trajectories of action forming the basis of a game exceeding individual limits. The most important thing is that these trajectories imply a progression towards greater purity – a progression following the development of the student's *karma*, and therefore the development of *dharma* itself as a general form. But there are possible exceptions to this progression: since the *dharma* of the authorities is to punish whenever purification is insufficient, or even inappropriate, this may lead to other forms of punishment. In their punishment task, however, the authorities cannot forget that they are themselves inscribed in a space of development that is entirely traversed by study; their task of surveillance and punishment only has meaning as anomalous to study, but as anticipated by that very study.

*

§77. *Artha.* The subordinate position of the authorities (the king in particular) in the system of *smriti*, is explained by the fact that their activities, while being connected to *dharma*, fell within the ambit of *artha*. As such, they were categorized in terms of work or profit, and occupied a subsidiary position with respect to study, even though integrated with it; in a certain respect, the same went for the punishments proceeding from it. Where the *Dharmasutra* focused primarily on forms of punishment rooted in contrition, the 'threads' of the *artha* entailed a violence that was *sui generis*, fully justifying its reference to the 'stick'. Book IV of the *Arthashastra*, attributed to Kautilya, a mythical minister of the emperor Chandragupta, and the only treatise on the *artha* to come down to us, envisaged a strict accounting of the price to be paid for a crime or infraction. This was effectively a general economy of cruelty, embracing the selection of ministers, courtly life and the administration of relations with other states, based on the cold calculation of power relations likely to lead to victory. This was hardly surprising: whatever his social standing, the king was first and foremost a warrior – the *dharma* of his caste compelled him towards violent action, and to scrupulous respect for the precepts the Brahmins had drawn from the tradition. *Artha* was his *dharma*; it was the form of action that *dharma* took in his case, inasmuch as he had a monopoly in the administration of punishments when these were separated from the strict logic of penitence. Which meant that royal power, as such, the authority of the one attending to people's behaviour, was a weak form of power, with respect to which the Brahmins found themselves in a position of theoretical superiority. Decreeing rules or applying punishments were degraded forms of study – or rather forms of study that only participated in *dharma* to the extent that they also worked towards its preservation. This, however, was not a foregone conclusion: it might happen that *artha*, like *karma*, was in conflict with the development of *dharma* – in which case, the king became a danger to be guarded against.

*

§78. Varna.   Contrary to a still common misconception, the system of *dharma* passed on by the *smriti* was anything but rigid, with hierarchies fixed for eternity; its principal characteristic was in fact movement. *Dharma* itself, in all its different forms (cosmic, ritual, *varna* or individual), continually flowed from the most singular to the most general, just as any practice could, at one time or another, become study. The four *varna* were themselves characterized by the fact that they ensured that *dharma* was deployed in a differentiated way, circulating amongst the 'castes' according to the rhythm of the actions in which their members engaged. The 'castes' as such, moreover, had nothing fixed about them: the revelation, as summarized in the *Bhagavadgita*, maintained that each *varna* was to be defined according to what it accomplished, and not what it was. It was not the natural order that determined membership of a caste, but the kind of actions by which an individual distinguished himself in the task of strengthening *dharma* – and therefore the kind of result that these actions were likely to have. Even though sanctions played a decisive role in a student's development, the aim was not to stop him or slow him down; like the actions themselves, the important thing was what they made possible. Rather

than being closed and rigid, the traditional system of ancient India was an engine of production; its primary goal was to save the world, not through the re-establishment of a former order, but through the establishment of a new equilibrium. Since the threat to the world is inscribed in the schema of an immense temporal cycle – in which we are living through the lowest age, the age of *Kali Yuga*, the 'age of Kali' or the 'age of vice' – only invention counts. In resisting *Kali Yuga*, anything that could work towards the strengthening of *dharma* counts – above all, what has not yet been conceived, what the tradition has not yet revealed, or what the Brahmins have not yet invented. *Smriti* is open, just like *dharma*, in that for each individual it finds the appropriate expression.

*

§79. *Manu.* In the centuries following the compilation of the *Dharmasutra*, however, the openness of *dharma* was challenged – as was the strict difference between the systems of sanctions connected with study and those connected with *artha*. The *Mānava Dharmaśāstra*, known in Western Europe as the 'Laws of Manu', exemplified this twofold change; its composition, during the second century CE, responded to a desire to unify the tradition within a rigid order. Unlike the *Dharmasutra*, the Laws of Manu incorporated precepts relating to study, rules concerning judicial procedure, the exercise of royalty as well as state administration. Inspired particularly by the *Gautama Dharmasutra*, the oldest of the *Dharmasutra*, the first seemed, on the face of it, to be limited to a reformulation of essential teachings. With the second, the anonymous author of the Laws did not conceal the extent to which their reformulation was based on observations developed by Kautilya in his *Arthashastra*: he had no desire for originality in this sphere either. Besides its stylistic innovations (the 'Laws' were written in the form of a verse dialogue between 'Manu' and an audience rather than as a collection of aphorisms), its originality lay in the association of the two systems of order. By including the concerns of *artha* and *dharma* in the same work, he hoped to indicate the need for a new alliance between the Brahmins and the royal authorities – with relations between them having cooled. This alliance, however, meant an affirmation that called into question one of *dharma*'s most important considerations: the rigorous separation of class *dharma* from cosmic *dharma* – a separation noted, for those who were attentive, in Manu's discourse. After having expounded the history of the origin of the world, then described, in conformity with the *Dharmasutra*, the different sources of knowledge, he concluded by declaring that the time had come to study the *dharma* of the different classes. What had been united in study was now to be distinguished, as though knowledge was now to ally itself with power rather than with the world.

*

§80. *Asoka.* The moment that Right turns towards power is the moment it is lost: this is the risk the author of the Laws of Manu was, in full awareness, prepared to run in order to restore the status of Brahminic study. In doing so, he showed that he was prepared to accept that *dharma* could be divided up, leading to the weakening of the world; the circumstances of the age, however, demanded it. Three centuries before the composition of the Laws, Emperor Asoka had imposed a number of far-reaching reforms on India, allowing him to concentrate all power – be it political, juridical, military or moral – in his hands. During his reign, the 'officers of morality', the *Dhamma Mahāmātā*, criss-crossed the empire, tracking any failings by civil servants relating to the precepts of good behaviour he wanted to see respected. Even if his orders were driven by a desire to increase religious tolerance in a territory where Hinduism, Jainism and Buddhism fought over believers, the result was to diminish the role of Brahmins. From paragons of study, they found themselves demoted to the role of simple priests of just one religion among others; it was this secondary position that the author of the Laws claimed to reappraise by uniting the systems in the same *smriti* text. So, however unique his approach, his objective remained the preservation of the ideal of study espoused by the Brahmins from the beginning – and, particularly, the fact that there was no right *except* to study. Even the rules of policing that a prince like Asoka might decree should yield to the logic of study – to the fact that the precepts were always a point of departure for speculation, and never a destination. The *sutra* should allow for the invention of modes of action, rather than fixing them in a system that has been established once and for all; it was, after all, a question of saving the world from destruction. For the masters of study of classical India, the greatest fear was not insecurity or unpredictability, since both were typical of the cosmos; it was that the cosmos might disappear for once and for all.

INTERLUDE 8

§I. Judgement.   Since Law is so intimately bound up with sanction, we understand why it can only be actualized in judgement; to the extent that it is not used in judgement, Law is useless – it should even, no doubt, be revoked. This is because Law is conceived only according to the logic of immediate utility, of the instrument, of a tool in the service of institutions devised for the governance of human groups – serving, that is, to emphasize the respect they command. But the fact that this utility is revealed principally at the moment of judgement suggests that this respect is very fragile, and is only based on the expected coercive power of its application, once it has been delivered in accordance with the Law. The ideal of *isonomia* celebrated by the Greeks therefore takes on a new meaning: *isonomia* is not so much equality before an abstract *nomos* as equality before a concrete judgement – or, rather: before the order that this implies. *Isonomia* is equality before the obligation to obey; and the judgement is the primary operator of this equality – it is what enables the passage from the dream of sanction that defines Law to its realization at the level of government institutions. This is the only true creation likely to occur when judgement is enacted: the confirmation, in a given case, that it is possible to ensure that a sanction is agreed – and that Law, therefore, warrants its existence. From this point of view, a judgement creates nothing; it simply repeats, again and again, the incantatory gestures through which it is persuaded to apply meaning where there is none, and which it can only achieve by coercion. What, after all, does a judgement decide on if not the guilty – on the fact that someone, among the parties in a trial, must *pay* for what they have done, for having shown, that is, that Law was nothing without sanction? Judgement is not the application or interpretation of Law: it is the simple confirmation of its vengeful nullity, of its absence of justification, of its inability to produce anything. Judgement is the place where the absence of any Law reveals itself – the practical experience through which it reduces itself to the pure exercise of a sanction, ignorant of anything else.

9

MAÂT

§81. Maât. Most facts concerning the creation of the kingdom of Egypt remain unknown to us; the only thing we are sure of is that it came about through the unification of Lower and Upper Egypt in around the year 3000 BCE. According to Egyptian historiography, this unification, which created the first pharaonic dynasty, should be attributed to a certain Narmer, the first king of the first dynasty, about whom we know very little. Most of the sparse information we do have comes from a discovery made in 1897, in a Nekhen temple dedicated to the god Horus, by the English archaeologists James Quibell and Frederick Green, where they found a palette of greywacke more than sixty centimetres long, engraved on both sides and representing King Narmer exercising his powers surrounded by his tutelary gods. On the front, this power is demonstrated by the way in which he towers over the other engraved figures, and by a cameo showing two serpopards, symbolizing the two parts of unified Egypt. On the back, the king, occupying nearly the whole space, is shown threatening a kneeling man with his club – while the bottom part of the palette shows two bodies, which might be corpses or individuals about to be executed. On the one hand, the engraved motifs testified to the Pharaoh's organizing role; and, on the other, to his military activities – both with a view to establishing his authority within an order of which he was the guardian. More than a holder of power, the Pharaoh is its servant, since power here is not a tool to be used, but the condition for the continuation of an order extending to men and gods. With the discovery of the Narmer Palette, therefore, the fundamental coordinates of the pharaonic order revealed their origins: an order based on the power of an individual as well as the equilibrium he protected. If the king was a great guardian and great organizer, this was only so to the extent that his actions could be justified in the context of a principle that surpassed him – which the Egyptians called '*maât*'.

*

§82. *Ânkh.* In Egyptian iconography, Maât very early came to be represented as a young girl, her hair adorned with an ostrich feather, sporting different symbols depending on her posture – sitting down or standing up. Sitting on the ground or on a basket (*neb*), symbolizing totality, she most often holds in her hands the hieroglyph *ânkh*, signifying 'life'; when standing, or sitting on a throne, she also leans on a sceptre (*ouas*), the symbol of power. This symbol, associated with certain divinities, is also connected with the king: it is he who usually demonstrates his dominance in this way – and we are to understand that this is not alien to the figure of Maât. In its written form, '*maât*' uses two hieroglyphs, each connected to a particular characteristic: the pedestal, signifying stability and referencing the royal or divine throne (on which, therefore, she sometimes sits); and the feather, evoking the skies above. These representations very quickly became associated with the idea of *maât*, to the point that, in the era of the New Kingdom (and more precisely between the sixteenth and thirteenth centuries BCE), they gave rise, at the Pharaohs' request, to an official cult. As an explanatory principle of the cosmic order within which the king played an interfacing role, Maât had become a divinity in her own right – without, however, her primary function being substantially altered. From the end of the fourth to the beginning of the first millennium BCE, it always entailed something like an equilibrium – that which enabled stability in the relationship between gods and men. This all-encompassing stability did not, however, imply a structure to be defended; but rather, once it has been conceded that the equilibrium could only be vital, the way in which 'life' (*ânkh*) was to be organized. For a long time, the king was the exclusive guardian of this equilibrium – but, during the Middle Kingdom, it became the concern of every stratum of society, ultimately coming to constitute an essential dimension. *Maât* was no longer something the king said; it penetrated his words and actions, just as it did those of every other individual; having been the incarnation of *maât*, he was now only its institutional face.

*

§83. *Isfet*. '*In maât, der isfet*' ('he brings *maât*, and rejects *isfet*'): such was the king's mission – a mission to be understood in the framework of a play of antagonistic forces, where it was essential that *maât* prevailed. On the one side was order, peace, life, equilibrium, stability, prosperity, justice, equity and truth, while on the other there was disorder, war, death, disequilibrium, chaos, poverty, iniquity, injustice and lies. When *isfet* triumphed, the structure of the world collapsed and the divinities weakened, but when *maât* ruled, the cosmic, social and individual universe would thrive. In either case, what declared itself a principle of order or disorder involved much more than good policing of the city: not only was the destiny of the whole cosmos decided here, but the means by which this came about were many and varied. The principle guaranteed by the king was at the same time religious, moral, political, economic, epistemological, and so on; both *maât* and *isfet* encompassed the totality of dimensions of what was. Order was not limited to the governance of bodies, nor even to the conduct of souls; it incorporated the very texture of the world, and the possibility of guaranteeing its truth – the true was a dimension of the just, and vice versa. Connecting all these dimensions was the idea of *ânkh*, of life, which was always displayed in representations of the goddess: to assure the order of the world was to assure the possibility of the continuation of life. Which is why, of the different attempts to define *maât*, Bernadette Menu's is undoubtedly the most accurate: according to her, it refers to 'the totality of conditions that give rise to and renew life'. As a principle of order, *maât* is a principle of life; as a principle of life, it is a principle of truth; as a principle of truth, it is a principle of justice – a justice that is simultaneously cosmic, social and individual. When the king was expected to 'bring *maât* and reject *isfet*', it was this concern for the cultivation of life that he was to demonstrate, conveyed through the totality of the administrative, political and bellicose acts associated with his office.

*

§*84. Oasien.* The king, however, was not the only one
who had to demonstrate his attachment to *maât*; even at
a time when it had not yet given rise to a cult, its quality
as a principle of life meant it linked anyone involved in
the administration of life. Meaning it linked pretty much
everyone – since all the dimensions of what was were
answerable to the necessities of life and required behaviour
in accordance with them. A text from the time of the
Middle Kingdom, known as *The Eloquent Peasant* [*Conte
de l'Oasien*], provides a revealing example of the depth at
which *maât* was integrated into contemporary Egyptian
society. The text belongs to the 'grievance' genre of
literature, a genre dedicated to the examination of cases in
which the lack of *maât* enables a reflection on its necessity
for the operation of social life. The tale tells the story of a
poor peasant assaulted by the major-domo of a territory
he is crossing with his donkey, and who complains to
the territory's high steward – who asks him to provide
witnesses in support of his allegations. No one saw the
attack, but his eloquence fascinates the high steward, who
decides to write to the king, who orders him by return to
detain the peasant so that he might produce other wonders
of discourse. The peasant, who believes he is being
manipulated, loses patience, which earns him a beating
from the high steward; so he leaves the territory – before
being caught and brought back before the high steward,
who finally rewards him. Just when he loses patience,
the peasant indulges in an exercise of rhetorical bravura,
during which he formulates nine 'grievances', ending with
a peroration suggesting the outlines of a general theory of
maât. 'There is no yesterday for the indolent / no friend
for he who is deaf to *maât* / no holiday for the greedy', the
peasant moans, defining *maât, a contrario,* as that which,
in any life, avoids indolence, deafness and greed. Meaning
that *maât*, as a principle of life, should be understood as
the totality of mechanisms creating solidarity between
individuals and enabling them to act such that they avoid
the threat of egotism.

*

§*85. Communication.* *Maât* was a regime that, even though it found its privileged incarnation in the figure of the pharaoh, constituted the domain within which everyone acted and spoke, since everyone was, in one way or another, indebted to every other life. This regime extended in two different ways, depending on whether it was relating to words or actions: from the perspective of the word, it tended towards truth; while from the perspective of doing, it tended towards justice. Speaking, from the perspective of *maât*, meant communicating, in the sense that there is no communication except in the form of a coupling of one phrase with another – of the creation of continuity in speech. Doing, on the other hand, meant acting in such a way that the consequences produced by any action could be associated with it, and that these consequences were as sensitive to the other as they were to the self. Meaning that *maât*, as a principle of life, could claim to be a principle of continuity conceived as solidarity extended in time – just like the cosmos itself for the Egyptians. Where other civilizations conceived of the cosmos according to its spatial extension, ancient Egypt privileged its temporal extension – the fact that it is the mechanism ensuring its continuity that *constitutes* the cosmos. *Life is time*: this was the brute theorem on which the logic of *maât* was based; the solidarity whose principle it furnished was nothing other than the principle of continuity in time, without which no life was possible. Which was why the values promoted by the eloquent peasant are articulated as a rejection of deafness, indolence and greed: by revoking a form of action, it is a question on each occasion of breaking continuity. Integration in time was, therefore, *maât*'s function, where *isfet* was realized through saying and doing that contributed to disintegration in time, to the progressive unravelling of what was. This integration in time was pushed so far that it even implicated life beyond life: as a principle of life, *maât* was also to be considered a principle of death – or, in any case, as a principle articulating the one with the other.

*

§86. *Tomb.* Since the Egyptian cosmos took the form
of extension in time, organized as life according to *maât*,
the question of continuity had to be asked when life came
to an end, making way for death. Indeed, with death, the
question arose as to the continued transmission of the
words and actions of the one who had lived – the creation
of vital continuity beyond the bounds of life. Another of
ancient Egypt's literary genres was dedicated to explaining
how this creation of continuity might operate: the literary
genre of tomb inscriptions – which also dated back to the
origins of royalty. The role played by these inscriptions was
important: through a biographical mapping showing that
he had indeed lived according to *maât*, it provided a kind
of justification for the existence of the one who had been
buried. It was a formulaic genre – but the stereotypical
nature of the lives it sketched only indicated the extent to
which, rather than their singularity, it was their participation in the circulation of solidarity that was important.
A life could continue into death only to the extent that it
had distinguished itself in solidarity, and that this did not
stop exerting its influence when existence was finished
– by way of heirs among other things. Through what is
only an apparent paradox, it was abandonment to the
neutrality of solidarity that provided the surest indication
of individual distinction – which offered proof of a life
led according to its principle. It was this proof that these
inscriptions sought to document, knowing that, according
to the rites of ancient Egypt, death meant judgement in the
form of a weighing of souls, a weighing of their quality.
In the *Egyptian Book of the Dead*, compiled in around
the sixteenth century BCE, this moment of weighing was
informed by two long lists of sins whose avoidance it
was necessary to confirm. These lists were arranged
around two crucial faults: deafness and greed – two of the
categories highlighted in *The Eloquent Peasant*; just as
maât was necessary for an individual's integration in social
life, so it was for existence in the spaces of the beyond.

*

§87. *Ba.* The king once again played a crucial role here. He was an agent of *maât*, but, at the same time, he was also the incarnation of the transition itself, of *ba*, the interface between the world of the living and that of the dead. The hieroglyph for '*ba*', a bird taking off, recalls that, as king, he was to ascend to the sky to unite with the sun god, *Ra*, before coming back down to the men confined in their 'tombs' to reanimate them. The tomb was not only human destiny, it was also the place from which man acceded to humanity – to the sphere of saying and doing according to *maât*, stimulated by the king passing between worlds. The concept of '*ba*', of 'liminality', defined the soul in its ability to travel from the world of the living to the world of the dead, or as belonging always already to both, since it emerges from the tomb only to one day return. Into this transitivity, *maât* introduces, therefore, the idea of a lifting of liminality, an increase in the necessary level required to pass from one world to the other, in such a way that this passage takes the form of an ascension. The judgement of souls, based on their adherence to *maât*, was a judgement on their right to go beyond the limits of simple human survival, to accede to the possibility of immortality, to the possibility of triumph over the tomb. As a result, we must add that *maât*, when considered from the perspective of cosmic order, is this intensification; it is the *qualification* of the cosmic order, the expression of what 'quality' means in it. To act or to speak according to *maât* is to act or speak better than can be expected of an ordinary human being; it is to confront the question of liminality everywhere that a potential problem of solidarity between individuals arises. The word 'triumph' synthesizes this qualitative jump: just as King Narmer had triumphed over his adversaries and unified what had been separated, to live according to *maât* was to triumph over survival, as an absence of quality. Triumph in the solidarity of *maât* is what justifies life from the perspective of the transition between life and death; it is what ensures that, at the moment of judgement, the soul will receive its due.

*

§88. *Âdja*. So, we understand why, despite not seeming particularly technical at first sight, *maât*, in ancient Egypt, was the principle governing the function of judging in the traditional sense of the term; that of jurisdiction. Judges were expected to conform to it, in the sense that their work did not involve applying a rule to a case, but verifying that the principle of solidarity had qualified the situation they were examining. This did not mean that their judgements entailed no norms; likewise, it did not mean that they only judged according to what we might call 'fairness'; rules existed, and *maât* entailed much more than fairness. But it happened that, in their quest for truth (rather than justice), the judges *listened* to the different parties, in the same way that the individual living according to the principle guarded against deafness, before distinguishing *maât* from *isfet* in a given case. To this extent, judging, in ancient Egypt, did not lead to any verdict on guilt or fault; the judges were content to declare a situation to be *maâty* or *âdja*, namely, 'in conformity with *maât*' or 'on the wrong path', 'in opposition'. The important thing was that, at the conclusion of the judgement, the weighing of the situation, the integration of what had disintegrated could take place – an integration that, in most areas, took the form of arbitration rather than sentencing. When a sentence decides [*tranche*], it contributes to disintegration; instead of deciding, it would be better to bind, to reconstitute the lost solidarity, restoring the values of mutual listening it implied. Such that, when the judgement declared one of the parties to be *maâty*, it acknowledged a triumph – but a triumph that, even though it implied the defeat of the other party, did not mean humiliation or revulsion. The Egyptian judicial order was not, as we too often hear, coercive; it was an order of liberation, understood as liberation from *isfet*, disequilibrium, chaos and violence. Which presented a new paradox: triumph was the triumph of equilibrium – if by 'triumph' we mean the unilateral defeat of one side by the other, it was the triumph of the absence of triumph.

*

§89. Hépou. *Maât* liberates; judgement liberates; and
the law liberates when, like everything else, it conforms to
the logic of *maât* – meaning it is inscribed within what Jan
Assman has called a 'sociogonic principle of solidarity'.
Which is why, when the time came for them to adjudicate
on a case that had been brought before them, the judges
were less interested in laws than in what happened – even
if, in ancient Egypt, there were a great many laws in
existence. Despite a diversity of style, form and object,
these laws were all gathered under one term: the word
'*hépou*', which can be roughly translated as 'regulation',
but which has its origins in geometry. According to the
Coffin Texts, a collection of tomb inscriptions from the
time of the Middle Kingdom, the cord (*hep*) was the tool
enabling the exact area measurement of the location of a
tomb to be built. The concept of 'regulation', *hépou*, carried
the double meaning of rectitude and measure, which is to
say, the care accorded to the planning of the place reserved
for eternity for the dead – the place where their transition
from one world to the other would happen. Depending on
its application, *hépou* could designate either a custom or
the decision of an authority, but the most important thing
was that each 'regulation' was subsequently confirmed by
the existing power; *hépou* was invested with the force of
authority. So, it was not surprising that the same word,
'*hep*', designated both the binding force of a contract and
the jurisprudential decision that had become a precedent
to follow in subsequent matters. The act by which 'regulations' were confirmed was one of the duties of the
sovereign invested with *maât*; it was through the intermediary of *maât* that the *semen hépou* could take place – the
authority of a *hépou* being the authority of *maât* as such.
Similarly, the authority of a judgement or a contract could
only be considered effective if it participated in the cosmic
constitution of solidarity; on their own, respect for the
law or the terms of a convention had no power. For the
Egyptians, there was no law or contract unless it was just
and true; if not, they simply had not taken place.

*

§90. Nefer. The logic of *maât* was, therefore, a logic
deploying in a single movement an indivisible network
of motifs that were political, religious, ethical, juridical,
economic, anthropological, and so on. In the world
governed by *maât*, there was nothing that was not good,
that was not *nefer*; what was not good was not true, or just
or, no doubt, existent; what was not good drew strength
from the void and non-being. The fact that *nefer* designated the content of *maât* should therefore be understood
in a perspective that was anything but moral: the 'good'
was not a category of judgement, but a category of power.
nefer was the power of being or life, which structured the
world so as to make deployment against the opposing
forces of *isfer* possible – it was the power of constitution
in opposition to the power of destitution. That this power
was inscribed in the context of a royalty that was theoreti-
cally absolute might encourage us to think that it was just
an ideological fig leaf, barely concealing the operation
of an unequal society. Indeed, ancient Egypt was rigor-
ously structured, and tended to deny to the lower classes
the possibility of living according to *maât*; this refusal,
however, at the same time constituted the affirmation of its
omnipotence. That life according to *maât* should be denied
to some resulted from a number of contingent circumstances; but, as *The Eloquent Peasant* showed, these could
be lifted or even inverted. Indeed, at the end of the story,
the peasant, who had been mistreated by the supervisor of
the territory whom he had crossed in such an unfortunate
way, saw the latter punished with the revocation of all
his property, which was offered in compensation to the
peasant. *Maât* occasionally performed miracles even when
society proved forgetful of its importance – and behaved
as though *everything* in it did not depend on the principle
of solidarity expressed by *maât*. This principle of solidarity
was, however, crystal clear; it could even be formulated in
the form of a maxim reminiscent of a certain categorical
imperative: act only in such a way that little fish are not
eaten by bigger fish.

INTERLUDE 9

§*J. Politics.* Law is not a juridical device; it is a political device – the device by which politics is foreclosed by politics, reduced to the policing of bodies and the spaces they are believed to occupy. Law is the device by which the field of political possibilities is diminished to a constituted state of affairs; only one thing is expected of it: its most complete conservation possible. Meaning that, whatever 'progress' might be noted [*actées*] in its practice, Law is essentially *reactive*; it only serves to express what everyone knows already but is not entitled to consider evident. In other words: Law is the double rejection of the banal evidence of what is – and the inevidence of what could be, but which would require much more than a judgement or a sanction to exist. Since Law can only acknowledge, it is the sanction and the judgement that are to realize what it is incapable of making exist by itself – at least, in a non-declamatory mode. The only politics it is fit to serve is, therefore, the politics of the sanction – the politics of punishing what does not stay in place, since this place above all entails pledging allegiance to Law that formulates its order. The principal maxim for this politics might be: *what is legal is just* – or: what respects Law is just, it being understood that Law is the polite form of the threat levelled at those who would claim to want something other than what they are given. The just is the genteel form of paternalism, if you like; in any case, it is the name of an ideal whose dream properly belongs only to those in a position to maintain its more or less ordered deployment. The only justice that can be expected of Law is that of the order whose instrument it is, namely the continuation of the existing state of affairs by any means possible – which was what the Greeks wanted. Justice, for them, can only be stasis, where injustice is ecstasy [*extase*] – the exit from stasis, the exploration of a line of flight with respect to the homeostasis of order, disequilibrium of what was in equilibrium, and so on. Justice is policing; injustice is politics.

10

AGGADAH

§91. Torah.   The history of the Torah is a complicated one, where it is not certain that the different conclusions have ever been properly resolved – for one reason, because overly radical examinations are often badly received. It is, however, accepted that the compilation of the five books of the Pentateuch took place at the time of the forced exile of the Judeans in Babylon, where they had been driven in around 597 BCE by Nebuchadnezzar II. The reason for this compilation was simple: to give to the people of Juda a kind of foundational identity through which they could know who they were beyond their geographical and institutional references. The aim of the Torah, the 'teaching', was to assemble all the prescriptions, authorizations and interdictions the Judeans had received from God by the intermediary of Moses, to whom he was said to have given them. Even though the Torah is presented as a text of a juridical nature, it is not entirely constituted of questions of Right; besides the 'commandments' (*taryag mitsvot*), there are of course a great many narratives. It happened, however, that the interpretation of the commandments in the written Torah demanded of its readers considerable efforts in elaboration and commentary, which gave rise to a vast body of knowledge. For a long time, this knowledge was considered foreign to the Torah as such, to the point that it was threatened by the complexities of its transmission – so the doctors of the Torah authorized its written composition. This came to be called the 'Oral Torah', as opposed to the 'Written Torah', which was the divine teaching; it brought together all the interpretations formulated by the doctors, whose chain of transmission went right back to Moses himself. The 'Oral Torah' gave rise to two kinds of writings: the first, called Mishna, 'repetition', assembled the words of the masters, while the second, the Guemara, or 'study' in Armenian, was an original commentary on the Torah. In around the fifth century BCE, the two writings were brought together in a single composition, called the Talmud, or 'study' in Hebrew – a study which was divided between two great fields: the Halakha and the Aggadah.

*

§92. *Halakha.*   The 613 commandments that the doctors
of law (officially named 'rabbis' from the first century)
had included in the Torah did not in fact exhaust either
its meaning or its contents. As well as the Halakha, the
logic of the commandments every Jew was expected to
respect, there was also, therefore, a vast body of material
that was not part of the exposition of 'Law', which was
called 'Aggadah'. This included historical, medical and
zoological observations, ethical teachings and the parables
and allegories of the sages – so everything that could not
be considered either a debate or a juridical decision. The
division of the two was, however, ambiguous, since the
Halakha did not so much designate a certain state of
the legislation as a trajectory or movement, embodied in
exemplary fashion by the idea of transmission. 'Halakha',
in Hebrew, comes from the verb '*halakh*', meaning 'to
walk': more than law, as such, it indicated a 'path' – the
one that, if the book of Exodus is to be believed, the
Jewish people were to take. Similarly, 'Aggadah' meant
'narrative', but in the very broad sense of 'anything that
can be told', provided this narration took place in a
didactic framework – so, by way of an adjuvant to the
normal instruments for the study of the law. In either case,
however, the insistence on the legalist dimension of the
Torah, even in its most unexpected manifestations, such
as, for example, the stories of witchcraft related in the
Aggadah, was to be qualified. The totality of rabbinical
knowledge in fact turned on the question of the commandments and how they were to be obeyed; yet this question,
in the eyes of the sages, could not be treated as implying
the simple following of rules. Rather than observation,
the Torah demanded *loyalty*: suggesting that the response
of each to the foundational commandments of the Jewish
religion should demonstrate first and foremost the piety of
the individual. *The law is the place of faith*: it is in its text
that the living heart of religiosity was to be found, even
if, the revelation having taken place once and for all, God
himself played only an incidental role.

*

§93. Justification. Since the Torah is the seat of faith, it is
not surprising that the Halakha draws no authority from
it; it has at its disposal no device by which it can even
ensure respect, other than its association with the Jewish
community. Its force is purely declarative – it is based only
on the long chain of transmission along which the rabbis
return to the source of all faith and are able to justify the
precepts in the lives of the faithful. As opposed to the rules
of Right, whose formulation always takes apodictic form,
the commandments of Halakha are always presented as
justificatory; they declare their reason for being within
their demands. So, one of the commandments formulated
in the book of Exodus stipulates: 'Honour your father
and mother (commandment), so that you may live long in
the land the Lord your God is giving you (justification).'
The history of Talmudic Right, from the moment God fell
silent, consists in the examination of these justifications,
or in their deeper exploration where they are lacking or
where they are too obscure to be understandable. The
Halakha is not the analysis of normative statements, but
the construction of the justifications it is possible to give
them; it is not a finite number of rules that is being trans-
mitted, but an infinite number of explanations. With time,
these have benefited from the development of many sources
of interpretation, including, amongst others, the *Minhag*
(usage), the *Sevarah* (logic), the *Ma'aseh* (example), the
Cheelot ou-techouvot (questions and responses), etc. The
hermeneutic practice as such, moreover, has been subject
to close regulation in response to the distinction between
the four possible meanings of law: literal (*pechat*), allusive,
Midrashic or esoteric (*sod*). Taken together, these sources
and techniques have enabled the doctors of law to
elaborate the monumental system of justification that is
the Talmud, understood as a system of *persuasion* – where
it is normally Right that is rooted in rhetoric. In every
gesture of existence, the path to be followed by the Jew is
a path that is justified, or it is not the path.

*

§94. *Maimonides.* In the *Guide for the Perplexed* (*More Nevoukhim*), composed by Maimonides in Arabic in around 1190 when he was living in Fostat in the suburbs of Cairo, it is possible to find a concise justification of justification. 'The general object of Law is twofold,' writes Maimonides, 'the well-being of the soul, and the well-being of the body. The well-being of the soul is promoted by the correct opinions communicated to the people according to their capacity ... The well-being of the body is established by a proper management of the relations in which we live one to another.' If each commandment must be justified, it is because together they rest on a funda-mental principle, in the light of which everything must be measured – a principle that is not that of religious or juridical orthodoxy. Law makes you think and law makes you live together – or, rather: the law makes you think *better* and live together *better*; its ultimate justification is not the acceptance of what is, but its improvement, its perfection in every respect. Maimonides continues: 'Of these two objects, the one, the well-being of the soul, or the communication of correct opinions, comes undoubtedly first in rank, but the other, the well-being of the body ... is anterior in nature and time.' The justification of justifi-cation belongs to the sphere of thought, even if, from the perspective of the history of man, the second objective has always presented greater urgency – because study is not possible without cohabitation. *There is no harmony of bodies except with a view to the perfection of the soul*: this was the maxim that Maimonides contends is ultimately justified by the doctrinal construction of the Talmud. When he put forward his own compilation of the rabbinic tradition, the *Mishneh Torah*, written between 1170 and 1180, it was to this requirement for the bettering of thought that he devoted his efforts. The title of the first part of the *Mishneh Torah*, 'Book of Knowledge', itself makes this explicit: to follow the teachings of the Halakha is to travel in the direction of knowledge, which is the last possible word of Law.

*

§95. *Chaim.* In order to orient themselves in the tangle
of commandments, the doctors of the Torah elaborated
a series of distinctions, which came to be added to the
classification of sources and the methods of interpretation.
The most important of these being the one separating
commandments of a 'monetary' nature (*diné mamonot*)
from those relating to the 'forbidden and permitted' (*issur
ve-hetter*), to the sphere of the religious strictly speaking,
that is. This was a very old distinction, preceding the
time when the title of Rabbi became official, and which is
thought to have been formalized at the end of the compilation of the *Mishna* in around the year 190. Monetary
Halakha concerns all commandments relating to obligations, whether they be contractual or delictual, while
the 'forbidden and permitted' concerns sacrifices, food,
agriculture and family. Despite the disparate nature of
this distinction, we should draw from it a very important
lesson, recalled by Chaim of Volozhin in the eighteenth
century: that the Halakha sought to cover every aspect
of Jewish life. *Everything is Halakha*: since Law is the
site of faith, and this must lead to the knowledge of what
is, in that what is has been conceived in its entirety by
God, we must realize that no sphere can escape Law. A
crucial corollary here is that, in this everything, we must
include what no longer, not yet, or does not at all, exist,
because Creation is not limited to a particular state of the
knowable; this is the everything to be known. The path of
Halakha is the path towards the knowledge of everything,
because only everything can be the *terminus ad quem* of
the work of perfecting the soul; to give up on everything,
therefore, is to give up on Law. That this everything
should be expressed in a finite number of commandments
presented no problem for Chaim, or for the doctors who
came before him: it fell to knowledge to constitute this
everything as such. Indeed, saying that the everything was
Halakha meant that it was Halakha that was everything,
and not the other way around: the revelation having been

given, infinitude is deployed by the interpretive knowledge
of those attempting to understand it.

*

§96. *Beyond.* Since everything is Halakha, even the
inexistent or the impossible, it is self-evident that the
extension of knowledge it necessitates produces consequences that exceed traditional normativity – in the
deontic sense. Indeed, the three operators of deontic
logic (the necessary, the permitted and the forbidden) are
incapable of accounting for the extent of the behavioural
register implied by the Torah, which includes both recom-
mendation and disapproval. Beyond these variants, it is the
extension of the context described by commandment that
is required by the total horizon of Halakhic knowledge –
an extension embodied in the principle *lifnim mi-shurat
ha-din*, 'beyond the limits of the law'. *The law says
always more than the law*: on the one hand, it is always
possible to apply it to cases it had not anticipated; while,
on the other, it is always possible to infer other kinds of
behaviour from it. Indeed, the most important thing is
that this serves study – that it allows for the imagining of
hypotheses that, even though there is no possibility they
will happen, still represent lessons open to potentially
useful meditation. This definition of Halakha as a universe
of hypotheses explains why, just as the normal limits of
juridical reasoning do not apply here, it privileges the
irresolute over the resolute. A hypothesis that has given
rise to a solution is not useful as a hypothesis; its only use
is now in its ability to produce, through interpretation,
other hypotheses leading to other interpretations, and so
on. On the other hand, a case that is still open is an inter-
pretational accelerator: it is not consensus that enables
knowledge but controversy – disagreement on how a
case should be resolved. This is because the only effect
of a solution, in itself, is to *settle* what should remain
open for eternity; you cannot settle everything, you can
only explore it endlessly, and abstain from deciding what

cannot be decided. Such that, the fact that anything might be true belongs to the logic of Halakha: every proposed solution of a hypothesis has the same burden of truth as any other – and the eventual choice of one of them does not mean the disqualification of the others.

*

§97. *Pluralism. Everything is true*: such is the fundamental maxim of Talmudic Right – everything is true, because everything is possible; but this possibility is expressed as a hypothesis of knowledge; so, Halakha is the knowledge of everything, as always true. Since everything is true, it must be understood that the different circumstances that could impose a limitation on the totality, as on truth, are null and invalid: everything is true, always and forever. Which also means that everything can be true at the same time, without this inconsistency or paradox causing any problem beyond the simple management of local consequences: as such, inconsistency and paradox are instructive. It is, therefore, perfectly acceptable for a given solution to a given hypothesis to be simultaneously correct and incorrect, right and wrong, since they both belong to the infinite sphere of creation as explored by knowledge. A famous *midrash* from the Eruvin tractate of the Babylonian Talmud explains this through a story: 'For three years Beit Shammai and Beit Hillel disagreed. The first said: The law is in accordance with our opinion, and the second said: The law is in accordance with our opinion. Ultimately, a Divine Voice emerged and proclaimed: both are the words of the living God. However, the law is in accordance with the opinion of Beit Hillel. Since both are the words of the living God, why were Beit Hillel privileged to have the law established in accordance with their opinion? The reason is that they were agreeable and forbearing, and when they taught the law, they would teach both their own statements and the statements of Beit Shammai. Moreover, when they formulated their teachings and cited a dispute, they prioritized the statements of Beit

Shammai over their own.' Halakhic pluralism was what justified the supremacy of one school over the other: the one that showed that even opinions contrary to their own were rooted in the true inevitably got the better of those who thought otherwise. But, everything being true, why did this last opinion deserve disqualification? The answer is simple: if there is only knowledge of everything, opinions that arrest the movement of everything do not belong to knowledge; they belong to another sphere, of which the doctors need know nothing.

*

§98. *Mishpatim.* There is, however, an acknowledged limit to the Halakha's authority; this limit is found in the 'laws' section (*Mishpatim*) of the book of Exodus – the section in which God delivers a first series of commandments to Moses. In the first verse of Chapter 21, the following words are spoken by God: 'Now these are the *Mishpatim* that you shalt set before them', namely, the Hebrews, considered the only chosen people. By '*Mishpatim*', therefore, we should understand 'laws', 'ordinances', 'decrees' or 'statutes', which is to say, all the official instruments through which the divine *Halakhot* come to be formulated, while not being reducible to them. The word '*Mishpatim*', moreover, could also be translated as 'disputes' or 'judicial actions': the Hebrews are to follow the 'laws' taught by God, with these teachings being also matters of business. Halakha is therefore knowledge of everything expounded by the commandments, inasmuch as this knowledge is displayed in the hypothetical exploration of disputes – particularly the most banal disputes. Maimonides is very insistent on this: law should be primarily concerned with the ordinary, the everyday; the exceptional should be exceptional, and not constitute its normal sphere of operation. The everyday here is, however, the everyday of the chosen people, and of them alone; as a result, the only limit to apply to the realm of the Halakha is a limit *ratione personae*, obliging the believer to turn only to the tribunal their faith. Rationally, nothing was more obvious: once it had been accepted that only Halakhic knowledge was knowledge of everything, it had to be concluded that all the others could only offer partial knowledge. Keeping to the juridical limit that a Jew could only have recourse to a Rabbinic tribunal was the necessary condition for retaining the possibility of knowledge of everything: the limit determines everything. The fact that the only possible everything was grafted on a limit explained the link with the true – because the true in question was in large part (that of Creation) beyond the reach of the official masters of interpretation.

*

§99. *Aggadah*. One might well wonder, however: if everything is Halakha, and if this entails that, within the limits of Hebraic jurisdiction, everything is true, what should we conclude as to the status of Aggadah – still a significant part of the Talmud? For a long time, the doctors of law hesitated over this: from their perspective, the Aggadah seemed to be too much of a composite, too far from the formal rigour of the commandments to be considered as belonging to the law strictly speaking. The fact that it was part of the revelation, however, meant that there must have been something to it, just as the definition of everything as an ecology of Halakha suggested that they were not without connection. It had to be acknowledged, therefore, that the Aggadah was also Halakah – that the stories and parables, the medical and zoological considerations, and the folk traditions were integrated into the body of the law, into the ecology of the commandments. This integration was rendered possible in two ways: first, through the development of the Midrashic method, making almost exclusive use of narrative; and second, through the progressive compilation of the Aggadah by the doctors themselves. In the fifteenth century, the *Ein Yaakov* ('Jacob's Well'), by the Spanish Rabbi Jacob ibn Habib, for the first time presented believers with a vision

of the Talmud in which only the Aggadic teachings were
retained. This inaugurated a lasting tradition, whose
modern masterpiece comes from the work of Hayyim
Nahman Bialik, the great reformer of Jewish poetry,
who in 1910 published a new anthology titled *Sefer
HaAggadah*. Between the two, the Aggadah had come to
be recognized for what it was: a perspective on the Torah,
just like the Halakha – a perspective encompassing everything in a similar way to the latter. Because, if everything
is Halakha, but the Aggadah is also Law, it follows that
everything is Aggadah as well; but from a different point of
view – from a place authorizing the proliferation of interpretations. As Bialik himself emphasized in a short essay
written in Odessa in 1915, 'In fact, *Halakha* and *Aggadah*
are one, they are two aspects of the same creature', two
modes of creation.

*

§100. *Betrayal.* Halakah is Aggadah; Aggadah is
Halakha; the one and the other are true and are modes
by which to apprehend everything, in that everything,
provided it concerns the Jewish people, issues from
commandment. When it comes to knowledge, the story
is as good as the rule; the only condition they both must
satisfy is that of the production of new knowledge,
contributing to the perfection of thought. In linking
Halakah, Aggadah and creation, Bialik indicated the
necessity of this condition: if knowledge can only be
expressed in terms of its relation to everything, then this,
as infinite, implies a continual creation. Repeating the
Torah is not enough: the commandment only has meaning
when it is surpassed, exceeded by the knowledge that
deploys it where it had no business – where its hypothesis
or justification can be transformed. Through the play of
Halakha and Aggadah, Law disseminates, proliferates and
ramifies; it ceaselessly moves away from the consistency,
coherence and unity of order, to accede to the hypothetical
infinity of everything. Which is why it is doubtless possible

to argue that Halakha and Aggadah, as perspectives on the Law, are two modes of betraying the Torah – two ways of contradicting it in order to respect it better. Translating the word 'Torah' by the word '*nomos*' is, therefore, a clumsy mistake: unlike the Torah, *nomos* demands that we focus on it, that we ceaselessly return to it. The Torah, on the other hand, demands nothing, but opens the possibility of divergence from it; it is Law that refuses to behave as Law, giving free rein to a liberated and savage creation of hypotheses, even if they are impossible. Rather than an incarnation of *nomos*, the Torah is, therefore, its opposite: it is what endlessly belies the pretentions of *nomos* to rule over everything, to the benefit of an endless 'movement', or a 'story' whose paths are always invited to bifurcate. But history is cruel: moving and telling, as creative operations, are precisely what *nomos* has sought to control from any quarter, without this amounting to anything but the proliferation of ways and fantasies, paths and fictions.

POSTLUDE

§K. Right. After Law, there is Right; after Law, there is everything that was consigned to oblivion by Law; there is invention and disorder, knowledge and exploration, multiplicity and singularity, being and things, the power of gestures and words. After *lex*, there is *ius*, *li*, *giri*, *dharma*, *fiqh*, *aggadah*, *maât* and *dînum*; after *nomos*, there is anomy, anarchy, injustice, arbitrariness, casuistry, magic, story, religion and ritual. After Law are all the means humans have invented to *become* rather than *be*, and to cause to become along with them the relations that unite them with others and bring them together in groups. This is the main difference that separates Law from Right: Law only knows being, a being it is committed to defending through its structure and function – a being it is its duty not to challenge. While the different appearances Right has assumed throughout the ages in order to shield itself from the temptation of Law, and to preserve something of the efficacity of its mechanisms, have had the opposite aim, however varied. It has been dedicated to the invention of always novel modalities for the transformation of what is – the logical *design* of possibilities contained in the existing state of affairs, that it could not ignore except by coercion. Where Law has always been conservative, Right has always been revolutionary, understood as the eternal return of the different, which, in coming back, endlessly diverges from what was before. *The only Right*

is revolutionary – permanent, continuous, persistent revolution, provided it is admitted that only what transforms itself persists, that there is only being as becoming. The excessive dimension of this becoming is worked by Right, as that which bears always more than itself in its movement – the individual bears relations, each relation bears others, and so on. *Right is the logistics of excess*; it is the chaotic organization of the aberrant becomings of the individual, whether human or not, existing only in the unstable game of connections through which it alters the ecology of the relations within which it is inscribed. After Law, perhaps we will manage to relearn the rules.

Notes

Prelude

§A. – On the concept of the real: Jacques Lacan, *The Seminar of Jacques Lacan IX: Identification*, trans. Cormac Gallagher from unedited French manuscripts (London: Karnac Books, 2002); Alenka Zupancic, *Ethics of the Real. Kant with Lacan* (London: Verso, 2000); Slavoj Zizek, *The Most Sublime Hysteric: Hegel with Lacan* (Cambridge: Polity, 2014); Massimo Recalcati, *Il vuoto e il resto. Il problema del reale in Jacques Lacan* (Milan: Mimesis, 2013); Alain Badiou, *À la Recherche du réel perdu* [*In Search of the Lost Real*] (Paris: Fayard, 2015). See also Laurent de Sutter, *Théorie du kamikaze* [*Theory of the Kamikaze*] (Paris: PUF, 2016).

Chapter 1

§1. – On the contemporary Greek context: Pierre Lévêque, *The Greek Adventure*, trans. Miriam Kochan (London: Weidenfeld & Nicolson, 1968); Claude Mossé, *Histoire d'une démocratie. Athènes, des origines à la conquête macédonienne* [*History of a Democracy: Athens, From its Origins until the Macedonian Conquest*] (Paris: Seuil, 1971); Edmond Lévy, *Nouvelle Histoire de l'Antiquité, t. 2, La Grèce au Ve siècle. De Clisthène à Socrate* [*New History of Antiquity, vol. 2, Fifth-Century Greece: From Cleisthenes to Socrates*] (Paris: Seuil, 1995); François Lefèvre, *Histoire du monde grec antique* [*History of the Ancient Greek*

World] (Paris: LGF, 2007). – On Cleisthenes: Pierre Lévêque et Pierre Vidal-Naquet, *Clisthène l'Athénien. Essai sur le représentation de l'espace et du temps en Grèce de la fin du VIe siècle à la mort de Socrate* [*Cleisthenes the Athenian: Essay on the Representation of Space and Time in Greece from the End of the Sixth Century until the Death of Socrates*] (Paris: Macula, 1983). – On the concept of *isonomia*: Martin Ostwald, *Nomos and the Beginnings of Athenian Democracy* (Oxford: Clarendon Press, 1969); Jacqueline de Romilly, *La Loi dans la pensée grecque, des origines à Aristote* [*Law in Greek Thought, from the Origin until Aristotle*] (Paris: Les Belles Lettres, 1971); Kôjin Karatani, *Isonomia and the Origins of Philosophy*, trans. Joseph A. Murphy (Durham, NC: Duke University Press, 2017).

§2. – On the history of the concept of *nomos*: Louis Gernet, *Recherches sur le développement de la pensée juridique et morale en Grèce. Étude sémantique* [*Investigations into the Development of Juridical and Moral Thought in Greece. A Semantic Study*] (Paris: Ernest Leroux, 1917); Marcello Gigante, *Nomos Basileus* (Naples: Glaux, 1956); Martin Ostwald, *Nomos and the Beginnings of Athenian Democracy*, *op. cit.*; Jacqueline de Romilly, *La Loi dans la pensée grecque, des origines à Aristote*, *op. cit.* – On Solon: Werner Jaeger, *Paideia: The Ideals of Greek Culture. Vol. I. Archaic Greece: The Mind of Athens (1933–1947)*, trans. Gilbert Highet (Oxford: Oxford University Press, 1986); Moses I. Finley, *Economy and Society in Ancient Greece* (1953) (London: Chatto & Windus, 1981); Louis Gernet, *Droit et société en Grèce ancienne* [*Right and Society in Ancient Greece*] (Paris: Sirey, 1955); Claude Mossé, 'Comment s'élabore un mythe politique: Solon, "Père fondateur de la démocratie athénienne"' ['How to Create a Political Myth: Solon, "Founding Father of Athenian Democracy"'], *Annales 54* (1979), pp. 425–437; John D. Lewis, *Solon the Thinker. Political Thought in Archaic Athens* (London: Bloomsbury, 2008). – On the root *dhè–: Émile Benveniste, *Dictionary of Indo-European Concepts and Society*, trans. Elizabeth Palmer (Chicago: HAU Books, 2016).

§3. – On the *rhêtra*: Jacqueline de Romilly, *La Loi dans la pensée grecque, des origines à Aristote*, *op. cit.*; Françoise Ruzé, 'Le conseil et l'assemblée dans le grande rhètra de Sparte' ['The Council and the Assembly in the Spartan Great Rhetra'],

Revue d'études grecques 104/1 (1991), pp. 15–30; Edmond Lévy, 'La grande Rhêtra', *Ktèma* 2 (1997), pp. 85–103; Id., *Sparte. Histoire politique et sociale jusqu'à la conquête romaine* [*Sparta: Political and Social History until the Roman Conquest*] (Paris: Seuil, 2003); Jacqueline Christien et Françoise Ruzé, *Sparte. Histoire, mythes, géographie* [*Sparta: History, Myths, Geography*] (Paris: Armand Colin, 2017), 2nd edn.

§4. – On the root *nem–: Émile Benveniste, *Dictionary of Indo-European Concepts and Society*, *op. cit.* – On the connections between *nomos* and democracy: Martin Ostwald, *Nomos and the Beginnings of Athenian Democracy*, *op. cit.*; Moses I. Finley, *Politics in the Ancient World* (Cambridge: Cambridge University Press, 1983); Richard Garner, *Law and Society in Classical Athens* (London: Croom Helm, 1987); Mogens H. Hansen, *The Athenian Democracy in the Age of Demosthenes: Structure, Principles, and Ideology*, trans. J. A. Crook (Norman: University of Oklahoma Press, 1999); Claude Mossé, *Au Nom de la loi. Justice et politique à Athènes à l'âge classique* [*In the Name of the Law: Justice and Politics in Classical Athens*] (Paris: Payot, 2010).

§5. – On the connections between *nomos* and philosophy: Jacqueline de Romilly, *La Loi dans la pensée grecque, des origines à Aristote*, *op. cit.*; Pierre Aubenque, 'La loi chez Aristote' ['Law in Aristotle'], *Archives de philosophie du droit* 25 (1980), pp. 147–157; Kôjin Karatani, *Isonomia and the Origins of Philosophy*, *op. cit.*

§6. – On Heraclitus and *nomos*: Pierre Guérin, *L'Idée de justice dans la conception de l'univers des premiers philosophes grecs, de Thalès à Héraclite* [*The Idea of Justice in the First Greek Philosophers' Conception of the Universe, from Thales to Heraclitus*] (Paris: Alcan, 1934); Jacqueline de Romilly, *La Loi dans la pensée grecque, des origines à Aristote*, *op. cit.*

§7. – On the development of Greek Right: Louis Gernet, *The Anthropology of Ancient Greece*, trans. John Hamilton and Blaise Nagy (Baltimore, MD: Johns Hopkins University Press, 1981); Douglas M. MacDowell, *The Law in Classical Athens* (London: Thames & Hudson, 1978); Michael Gagarin, *Early Greek Law* (Berkeley: University of California Press, 1986). – On the concept of the *polis*: Mogens H. Hansen, *Polis and*

City-state: An Ancient Concept and its Modern Equivalent. Symposium, January 9, 1998 (Copenhagen: Munksgaard, 1998); Id., *Polis: An Introduction to the Ancient Greek City-state* (Oxford: Oxford University Press, 2006).

§8. – On the root *ar–: Émile Benveniste, *Dictionary of Indo-European Concepts and Society*, *op. cit.* – On *thémis* and *dikè*: Gustave Glotz, *La Solidarité de la famille dans le droit criminel en Grèce* [*Family Solidarity in Criminal Right in Greece*] (Paris: Albert Fontemoing, 1904); Michael Gagarin, 'Dikè in the Works and Days', *Classical Philology* 68 (1973), pp. 81–94; Id., 'Dikè in Archaic Greek Thought', *Classical Philology* 69 (1974), pp. 186–197; Eric A. Havelock, *The Greek Concept of Justice, from its Shadow in Homer to its Substance in Plato* (Cambridge: Harvard University Press, 1978); Marcel Detienne, 'Religions de la Grèce ancienne' ['Religions of Ancient Greece'] *École pratique des hautes études. Section des sciences religieuses. Annuaire* 99 (1990–1), pp. 243–246; Jean Rudhardt, *Thémis et les Hôrai. Recherches sur les divinités grecques de la justice et de la paix* [*Thémis and the Horae: Investigations into the Greek Gods of Justice and Peace*] (Geneva: Droz, 1999); Pierre Judet de la Combe and Barbara Cassin, 'Thémis', *Vocabulaire européen des philosophes* [*European Dictionary of Philosophers*], under the direction of Barbara Cassin (Paris: Seuil/Le Robert, 2004) pp. 1291–1296.

§9. – On *phusis* and the Sophists: Felix Heinimann, *Nomos und Physis. Herkunft und Bedeutung einer Antithese im griechischen Denken des 5. Jahrhunderts* (1945) (Basel: Friedrich Reinhardt, 1965); Mario Untersteiner, *The Sophists*, trans. Kathleen Freeman (Oxford: Basil Blackwell, 1954); George B. Kerferd, *The Sophistic Movement* (Cambridge: Cambridge University Press, 1981); Jacqueline de Romilly, *The Great Sophists in Periclean Athens*, trans. Janet Lloyd (Oxford: Clarendon Press, 1992); Gérard Naddaf, *L'Origine et l'évolution du concept grec de phusis* [*The Origin and Development of the Greek Concept of Phusis*] (Lewiston: Edwin Mellen, 1992); Barbara Cassin, *L'Effet sophistique* [*The Sophistic Effect*] (Paris: Gallimard, 1995).

§10. – On *politès*: Émile Benveniste, 'Two Linguistic Models of the City', in *Problems in General Linguistics*, trans. Mary Elizabeth Meek (Coral Gables, FA: University of Miami Press, 1971).

Interlude 1

§B. – On the 'door open to' argument: Isabelle Stengers, *La Vierge et le Neutrino. Les scientifiques dans la tourmente* [*The Virgin and the Neutrino: Scientists in Tourment*] (Paris: Les Empêcheurs de penser en rond/Seuil, 2006).

Chapter 2

§11. – On Hammurabi: Dominique Charpin, *Hammu-rabi de Babylone* [*Hammurabi of Babylon*] (Paris, PUF, 2003); Marc Van de Mieroop, *King Hammurabi of Babylon: A Biography* (London: Blackwell, 2005). – On the historical context: Leo Oppenheim, *Ancient Mesopotamia: Portrait of a Dead Civilization* (Chicago, IL: University of Chicago Press, 1964); Georges Roux, *La Mésopotamie* [*Mesopotamia*] (Paris: Seuil, 1995); Véronique Grandpierre, *Histoire de la Mésopotamie* [*History of Mesopotamia*] (Paris: Gallimard, 2010). – On the 'Code': *Le Code de Hammurabi* [*Hammurabi's Code*] (1973), ed. André Finet (Paris: Cerf, 2004), 5th edn; Jean Bottéro, 'Le "code" de Hammurabi' ['Hammurabi's "Code"'] (1982), in *Mésopotamie. L'écriture, la raison et les dieux* [*Mesopotamia: Writing, Reason and the Gods*] (Paris: Gallimard, 1987), pp. 284–334; Martha T. Roth, 'The Law Collection of King Hammurabi. Towards an Understanding of Codification and Text', in *La Codification des lois dans l'Antiquité. Actes du colloque de Strasbourg, 27–28 novembre 1997*, under the direction of Edmond Lévy (Paris: De Boccard, 2000), pp. 9–31; Béatrice André-Salvini, *Le Code de Hammurabi* [*Hammurabi's Code*] (Paris: Somogy, 2016).

§12. – On the concept of *mišarum*: Jean Bottéro, 'Le "code" de Hammurabi', *op. cit.*

§13. – On the discovery of the 'Code': Vincent Scheil, *La Loi du roi Hammourabi (vers 2000 av. J.-C.)* [*King Hammurabi's Law (around 2000 BCE)*] (Paris: Ernest Leroux, 1904), 2nd edn; Béatrice André-Salvini, *Le Code de Hammurabi, op. cit.* – On the concept of *dīnum*: Dominique Charpin, 'Le statut des "codes de lois" des souverains babyloniens' ['The Status of the Babylonian

Sovereigns' "Codes of Law"'], in *Le Législateur et la Loi dans l'Antiquité. Hommage à Françoise Ruzé* [*The Legislator and the Law in Antiquity: A Tribute to Françoise Ruzé*], under the direction of Pierre Sineux (Caen: PUC, 2005), pp. 93–108.

§14. – On the grammatical structure of the *šumma*: Jean Bottéro, 'Le "code" de Hammurabi', *op. cit.*; Martha T. Roth, *Law Collections from Mesopotamia and Asia Minor* (Atlanta: Scholars Press, 1995), 2nd edn. – On the divinatory tracts in Mesopotamia: Jean Bottéro, 'Divination et esprit scientifique' ['Divination and Scientific Spirit'] (1973), *Mésopotamie, op. cit.*, pp. 233–251; Pierre Villard, 'Divination et présages' ['Divination and Omens'], *Dictionnaire de la civilisation mésopotamienne* [*Dictionary of Mesopotamian Civilization*], under the direction of Francis Joannès (Paris: Robert Laffont, 2001), pp. 239–242.

§16. – On the method of variation: Jean Bottéro, 'Le "code" de Hammurabi', *op. cit.*; Martha T. Roth, *Law Collections from Mesopotamia and Asia Minor, op. cit.*; Dominique Charpin, 'Le statut des "codes de lois" des souverains babyloniens', *loc. cit.* – On *Šamaš*: Marie-Joseph Seux, *Hymnes et prières aux dieux de Babylone et d'Assyrie* [*Hymns and Prayers to the Gods of Babylon and Assyria*] (Paris, Cerf, 1976); Jean Bottéro, *La Plus Vieille Religion. En Mésopotamie* [*The Oldest Religion: In Mesopotamia*] (Paris: Gallimard, 1998); Francis Joannès, 'Šamaš', *Dictionnaire de la civilisation mésopotamienne, op. cit.*, pp. 813–815.

§17. – On the concept of *kittum*: Jean Bottéro, 'Le "code" de Hammurabi', *op. cit.*

§18. – On the functioning of the 'Code' as a model: Jean Bottéro, 'Le "code" de Hammurabi', *op. cit.*; Dominique Charpin, 'Le statut des "codes de lois" des souverains babyloniens', *op. cit.*

§19. – On Babylonian contract forms: Dominique Charpin, 'Les formulaires des contrats de Mari à l'époque amorrite, entre tradition babylonienne et innovation' ['The Contract Forms of Mari in the Amorite Era, between Babylonian Tradition and Innovation'], in *Trois Millénaires de formulaires juridiques* [*Three Millennia of Juridical Forms*], under the direction of Sophie Démare-Lafont and André Lemaire (Geneva: Droz, 2010) pp. 13–42.

§20. – On other juridical forms in the history of the Middle East: Guillaume Cardascia, *Les Lois assyriennes* [*Assyrian Laws*] (Paris: Cerf, 1969); Martha T. Roth, *Law Collections from Mesopotamia and Asia Minor, op. cit.*; *Rendre la justice en Mésopotamie. Archives judiciaires du Proche-Orient ancien (IIIe–Ier millénaires av. J.-C.)* [*Administering Justice in Mesopotamia: Judicial Archives of the Ancient Middle East (3rd–1st Millennium* BCE*)*], under the direction of Francis Joannès (Vincennes: PUV, 2000).

Interlude 2

§C. – On the history of the concept of code: Jacques Vanderlinden, *Le Concept de code en Europe occidentale du XIIIe au XIXe siècle. Essai de définition* [*The Concept of Code in Western Europe from the Thirteenth to the Nineteenth Century: Attempt at a Definition*] (Brussels: Éditions de l'Institut de Sociologie, 1967).

Chapter 3

§21. – On the 'Law': Paul-Frédéric Girard and Félix Senn, *Textes de droit romain* [*Texts of Roman Right*], vol. II, *Les Lois des Romains* [*The Laws of the Romans*] (Naples: Jovene, 1978), 7th edn; Alan Watson, *Rome of the XII Tables: Persons and Property* (Princeton, NJ: Princeton University Press, 1975); Michèle Ducos, *L'Influence grecque sur la loi des douze tables* [*The Greek Influence on the Law of the Twelve Tables*] (Paris: PUF, 1978); Marie Theres Fögen, *Histoires du droit romain. De l'origine et de l'évolution d'un système social* [*Histories of Roman Right: On the Origin and Development of a Social System*], trans. fr. Denis Trierweiler (Paris: Maison des sciences de l'homme, 2007). – On the concept of *rogatio*: Huguette Jones, *Introduction au droit romain* [*Introduction to Roman Right*], vol. I, *Sources formelles du droit romain* [*Formal Sources of Roman Right*] (Bruxelles: Kluwer, 1997). – On the historical context: Lucien Jerphagnon, *Histoire de la Rome antique. Les armes et les mots* [*History of Ancient Rome: Weapons and Words*] (Paris: Fayard, 1987); *Histoire romaine* [*Roman*

History], vol. I, *Des origines à Auguste* [*From the Origin until Augustus*], under the direction of François Hinard (Paris: Fayard, 2000); Mary Beard, *SPQR: A History of Ancient Rome* (London: Profile Books, 2015).

§22. – On the concept of *ius*: Alfred Ernout and Antoine Meillet, 'Ius', *Dictionnaire étymologique de la langue latine. Histoire des mots* [*Etymological Dictionary of the Latin Language: History of Words*] (1932) (Paris: Klincksieck, 1985), 4th edn, pp. 329–330; Pierre Noailles, Fas *et* Ius. *Études de droit romain* [Fas *and* Ius: *Studies in Roman Right*] (Paris: Les Belles Lettres,1948); André Magdelain, 'Le *Ius* archaïque' ['Archaic *Ius*'] (1983), *Jus Imperium Auctoritas. Études de droit romain* [Jus Imperium Auctoritas: *Studies in Roman Right*] (Rome: École française de Rome, 1990); Aldo Schiavone, *The Invention of Law in the West*, trans. Jeremy Carden and Anthony Shugaar (London: Belknap Press of Harvard University Press, 2012).

§23. – On the pontiffs: Aldo Schiavone, *The Invention of Law in the West*, op. cit.; Mario Bretone, *Histoire du droit romain* [*History of Roman Right*] (3rd edn, 1989), trans. fr. Luigi-Alberto Sanchi (Paris: Delga, 2016); Françoise Van Haeperen, *Le Collège pontifical (IIIe siècle av. J.-C. – IVe siècle apr. J.-C.). Contribution à l'étude de la religion publique romaine* [*The Pontifical College (3rd century* BCE *– 4th century* CE*): A Contribution to the Study of Roman Public Religion*] (Brussels/Rome: Institut historique belge de Rome, 2002); Jan Hendrik Vangaeren, *The Jurisdiction of the Pontiff in the Roman Republic. A Third Dimension* (Nijmegen: Wolf Legal Publishers, 2012); Michael Johnson, 'The Pontifical Law and the Civil Law: Towards an Understanding of the Ius Pontificium', *Athenaeum* 103/1 (2015), pp. 1410–1156. – On the archaic procedure: Paul-Frédéric Girard, *Manuel élémentaire de droit romain* [*Essential Guide to Roman Right*] (1929), ed. Jean-Philippe Lévy (Paris: Dalloz, 2003), 8th edn; Michel Villey, *Le Droit romain. Son actualité* [*Roman Right: How it Was*] (Paris: PUF, 1945); John M. Kelly, *Roman Litigation* (Oxford: Clarendon Press, 1966); Olga Tellegen-Couperus, *A Short History of Roman Law* (London: Routledge, 1993); Michèle Ducos, *Rome et le droit* [*Rome and Right*] (Paris: LGF, 1996); Ernest Metzger, *Litigation in Roman Law* (Oxford: Oxford University Press, 2005); Kaius Tuori, *The Emperor of Law: The Emergence of Roman Imperial*

Adjudication (Oxford: Oxford University Press, 2016). – On the concept of *fas*: Alfred Ernout et Antoine Meillet, 'Fas', *Dictionnaire étymologique de la langue latine, op. cit.*, p. 217; Jules Paoli, 'Le Monde juridique du paganisme romain' ['The Juridical World of Roman Paganism'], *Revue historique de droit français et étranger* [*Historical Review of French and Foreign Right*] 23 (1945), pp. 1–7; Pierre Noailles, Fas *et* Ius. *Études de droit romain, op. cit.*; Georges Dumézil, *Archaic Roman Religion*, trans. Philip Krapp (Chicago, IL: University of Chicago Press, 1970); Émile Benveniste, *Vocabulaire des institutions indo-européennes, op. cit.*

§24. – On *iura* and *iurare*: André Magdelain, 'Le *Ius* archaïque', *op. cit.*; Id., *De la royauté et du droit de Romulus à Sabinus* [*On Royalty and Right from Romulus to Sabinus*] (Rome, L'Erma' di Bretschneider, 1995).

§25. – On the *nexum*: Paul Huvelin, 'Magie et droit individuel' ['Magic and Individual Right'], *L'Année sociologique* 10 (1905), pp. 1–46; Paul-Frédéric Girard, *Manuel élémentaire de droit romain, op. cit.*; Henri Lévy-Bruhl, 'Nexum et mancipation' ['Nexum and Mancipation'], *Quelques problèmes du très ancien droit romain. Essais de solutions sociologiques* [*Some Problems in Very Ancient Roman Right: Attempts at Sociological Solutions*] (Paris: Domat-Montchrestien, 1934), pp. 138–154; Pierre Noailles, 'Nexum', *Revue historique de droit français et étranger* 20–21 (1940–1), pp. 205–274; Jean Gaudemet, 'Naissance d'une notion juridique. Les débuts de l'"obligation" dans le droit de la Rome antique' ['Birth of a Juridical Concept: The Beginnings of "Obligation" in Ancient Roman Right'], *Archives de philosophie du droit* 44 (2000), pp. 19–32. See also Laurent de Sutter, *Magic. Une métaphysique du lien* [*Magic: A Metaphysics of Connection*] (Paris: PUF, 2015). – On the procedure '*per aes et libram*': Paul-Frédéric Girard, *Manuel élémentaire de droit romain, op. cit.*; Henry Lévy-Bruhl, 'L'acte "*per aes et libram*"' ['The Act "*per aes et libram*"'], *Nouvelles études sur le très ancien droit romain* [*New Studies in Very Ancient Roman Right*] (Paris: Sirey, 1947), pp. 97–115; William Geddes, *Per Aes et Libram* (Liverpool: Liverpool University Press, 1952); Kaius Tuori, 'The Magic of Mancipatio', *Revue internationale des droits de l'Antiquité* [*International Review of the Rights of Antiquity*] 55 (2008), pp. 499–521.

§26. – On *civitas*: Émile Benveniste, 'Deux modèles linguistiques de la cité', *op. cit.*; Adrian N. Sherwin-White, *The Roman Citizenship* (Oxford: Oxford University Press, 1979), 2nd edn; Claude Nicolet, *Le Métier de citoyen dans la Rome républicaine* [*Being a Citizen in the Roman Republic*] (Paris: Gallimard, 1980), 2nd edn; Jane F. Gardner, *Being a Roman Citizen* (London: Routledge, 1993); Clifford Ando, *L'Empire et le Droit. Invention juridique et réalités historiques à Rome* [*Empire and Right: Juridical Invention and Historical Realities in Rome*], trans. fr. Michèle Bresson (Paris: Odile Jacob, 2013).

§27. – On the *Corpus Iuris Civilis*: Paul Collinet, *La Genèse du digeste, du code et des institutes de Justinien* [*The Genesis of the Digest: on Justinian's Code and Institutes*] (Paris: Larose et Tenin, 1952); Mario Bretone, *Histoire du droit romain*, *op. cit.*; Olga Tellegen-Couperus, *A Short History of Roman Law*, *op. cit.*; Huguette Jones, *Introduction au droit romain*, vol. I : *Sources formelles du droit romain*, *op. cit.*; Georges Tate, *Justinien. L'épopée de l'empire d'Orient* [*Justinian: The Epic of the Eastern Empire*] (Paris: Fayard, 2004); Aldo Schiavone, *The Invention of Law in the West*, *op. cit.*

§28. – On the *iurisprudentes*: Fritz Schultz, *History of Roman Legal Science* (Oxford: Clarendon Press, 1946); Peter Stein, *Regulae Iuris. From Juristic Rules to Legal Maxims*, (Edinburgh: Edinburgh University Press 1966); Mario Bretone, *Tecniche e ideologie dei giuristi romani* (Naples: ESI, 1985); Alan Watson, *The Spirit of Roman Law* (Athens: University of Georgia Press, 1995); Aldo Schiavone, *The Invention of Law in the West*, *op. cit.* – On the history of obligations in Roman Right: Alan Watson, *The Law of Obligations in the Later Roman Republic* (Oxford: Clarendon Press, 1965); Jean Macqueron, *Histoire des obligations* [*History of Obligations*], vol. I, *Le Droit romain* [*Roman Right*] (Aix-en-Provence: Faculté de droit et de sciences économiques, 1975), 2nd edn; Gyorgy Diosdi, *Contracts in Roman Law. From the Twelve Tables to the Glossators* (Budapest: Akademiai Kiado, 1981); Reinhard Zimmerman, *The Law of Obligations: Roman Foundations of the Civilian Tradition* (Oxford: Clarendon Press, 1997); Jean Gaudemet, 'Naissance d'une notion juridique. Les débuts de l'"obligation" dans le droit de la Rome antique', *op. cit.*

§29. – On Gaius: Gaius, *Institutes*, ed. Julien Reinach (Paris:

Les Belles Lettres, 1950); Fritz Schultz, *History of Roman Legal Science*, *op. cit.*; Anthony M. Honoré, *Gaius. A Biography* (Oxford: Clarendon Press, 1962); Aldo Schiavone, *Ius. L'invention du droit en Occident*, *op. cit.*

§30. – On satirizing juridical practice in end of the Republic Rome: Michèle Ducos, *Les Romains et la loi. Recherches sur les rapports de la philosophie grecque et de la tradition romaine à la fin de la République* [*The Romans and the Law: Investigations into the Relations between Greek Philosophy and the Roman Tradition at the End of the Republic*] (Paris: Les Belles Lettres, 1984).

Interlude 3

§D. – On the casuistic: *Penser par cas* [*Thinking by Case*], under the direction of Jean-Claude Passeron and Jacques Revel (Paris: Éditions de l'EHESS, 2005).

Chapter 4

§31. – On the relations the Romans maintained with Law: Michèle Ducos, *Les Romains et la Loi*, *op. cit.*; Alan Watson, *The Spirit of Roman Law*, *op. cit.* – On the *leges regiae*: André Magdelain, 'Le *Ius* archaïque, *op. cit.*; Id., *De la royauté et du droit de Romulus à Sabinus*, *op. cit.*; Huguette Jones, *Introduction au droit romain*, vol I, *Sources formelles du droit romain*, *op. cit.* – On the history of legislation at the end of the Republic: Olga Tellegen Couperus, *A Short History of Roman Law*, *op. cit.*

§32. – On the concept of *lex*: Alfred Ernout et Antoine Meillet, *Dictionnaire étymologique de la langue latine*, *op. cit.*, pp. 353–354; Émile Benveniste, *Vocabulaire des institutions indo-européennes*, *op. cit.*; André Magdelain, *La Loi à Rome. Histoire d'un concept* [*Law in Rome: History of a Concept*] (Paris: Les Belles Lettres, 1978); Jean-Pierre Beaud, 'Lex', *Vocabulaire européen des philosophes*, *op. cit.*, pp. 710–715.

§33. – On Cicero: Claude Nicolet and Alain Michel, *Cicéron* [*Cicero*] (Paris: Seuil, 1960); Pierre Grimal, *Cicéron* [*Cicero*]

(Paris: Fayard, 1986); Pierre-François Mourier, *Cicéron. L'avocat et la république* [*Cicero: The Lawyer and the Republic*] (Paris: Michalon, 1996); Clara Auvray-Assayas, *Cicéron* [*Cicero*] (Paris: Les Belles Lettres, 2006). – On the transformations of Roman society at the end of the Republic: Elizabeth Rawson, *Intellectual Life in the Late Roman Republic* (Baltimore, MD: Johns Hopkins University Press, 1985); Marcel Le Glay, *Rome. Grandeur et déclin de la République* [*Rome: The Grandeur and Decline of the Republic*] (Paris: Perrin, 1990).

§34. – On the *De Legibus*: Cicéron, *Traité des lois* [*Treatise on the Laws*], ed. Georges de Plinval (Paris: Les Belles Lettres, 1959); Michèle Ducos, *Les Romains et la loi*, *op. cit.*; Pierre Grimal, *Cicéron*, *op. cit.*; *Cicero's Law: Rethinking Roman Law of the Late Republic*, under the direction of Paul J. du Plessis, (Edinburgh: Edinburgh University Press, 2016).

§35. – On Cicero's juridical stoicism: Geneviève Rodis-Lewis, *La Morale stoïcienne* [*Stoic Morality*], (Paris: PUF, 1970); Michèle Ducos, *Les Romains et la loi*, *op. cit.*; Pierre Grimal, *Cicéron*, *op. cit.*; Pierre-François Mourier, *Cicéron. L'avocat et la république*, *op. cit.*; Carlos Lévy, *Les Philosophies hellénistiques* [*Hellenistic Philosophers*] (Paris: LGF, 1997); Olga Tellegen-Couperus and Jan Williem Tellegen, 'Reading a Dead Man's Mind: Hellenistic Philosophy, Rhetoric and Roman Law', in *Cicero's Law*, *op. cit.*, pp. 26–49.

§37. – On the great schools of *iurisprudentes* in second-century Rome: Fritz Schultz, *History of Roman Legal Science*, *op. cit.*; Aldo Schiavone, *The Invention of Law in the West*, *op. cit.* – On the *ius publice respondendi*: Olga Tellegen-Couperus, *A Short History of Roman Law*, *op. cit.*; Mario Bretone, *Histoire du droit romain*, *op. cit.*

§38. – On Cicero's influence on the subsequent development of Roman Right: Michèle Ducos, *Les Romains et la loi*, *op. cit.*; Alan Watson, *The Spirit of Roman Law*, *op. cit.*; Aldo Schiavone, *The Invention of Law in the West*, op. cit.

§40. – On Roman legislation at the end of the Empire: Mario Bretone, *Histoire du droit romain*, *op. cit.*; Olga Tellegen-Couperus, *A Short History of Roman Law*, *op. cit.* – On the fate of the concept of *lex* in the Western juridical tradition: Stig Strömholm, *L'Europe et le Droit* [*Europe and Right*], trans. fr.

Frédéric Durand (Paris: PUF, 2002); Peter Stein, *Roman Law in European History* (Cambridge: Cambridge University Press, 1999); Paolo Grossi, *L'Europe du droit* [*The Europe of Right*], trans. fr. Sylvie Taussig (Paris: Seuil, 2011).

Interlude 4

§E. – On the distinction between 'Sein' and 'Sollen': Hans Kelsen, *Pure Theory of Law*, trans. from 2nd (revised and enlarged) German edition by Max Knight (Berkeley: University of California Press, 1967); Carlos Miguel Herrera, *Théorie juridique et politique chez Hans Kelsen* [*Juridical and Political Theory in Hans Kelsen*] (Paris: Kimé, 1997); Pierre Hack, *La Philosophie de Kelsen. Epistémologie de la théorie pure du droit* [*The Philosophy of Kelsen: Epistemology of the Pure Theory of Law*] (Basel: Helbing & Lichtenhahn, 2004). – On the concept of the '*peut-être*': Laurent de Sutter, 'Les deux ontologies de Giorgio Agamben' ['The Two Ontologies of Giorgio Agamben'], forthcoming.

Chapter 5

§41. – On the origins of Islam: Albert Hourani, *A History of the Arab Peoples* (Cambridge, MA: Harvard University Press, 1991); Claude Cahen, *Islam. Des origines au début de l'Empire ottoman* [*Islam: From the Origins to the Beginning of the Ottoman Empire*] (Paris: Hachette, 1997); Sabrina Mervin, *Histoire de l'islam. Doctrines et fondements* [*History of Islam: Doctrines and Foundations*] (Paris: Flammarion, 2000); Alfred-Louis de Prémare, *Les Fondations de l'islam. Entre écriture et histoire* [*The Foundations of Islam: Between Writing and History*] (Paris: Seuil, 2002); *Les Débuts du monde musulman, VIIe–Xe siècle. De Muhammad aux dynasties autonomes* [*The Beginnings of the Muslim World, 7th–10th Century: From Muhammad to the Autonomous Dynasties*], under the direction of Thierry Bianquis, Pierre Guichard and Mathieu Tillier (Paris: PUF, 2012). – On Mohammad: Maxime Rodinson, *Muhammad*, trans. Anne Carter (London: Penguin, 1996), 2nd English edn; W. Montgomery Watt, *Muhammad: Prophet and*

Statesman (Oxford: Oxford University Press, 1964); Anne-Marie Delcambre, *Mahomet* (Paris: Desclée de Brouwer, 1999); Hichem Djaït, *The Life of Muhammad*, 3 vols., trans. Janet Fouli (Tunis: Tunisian Academy of Sciences, Letters, and Arts, Beit al-Hikma, 2014). – On the Koran: Régis Blachère, *Introduction au Coran* [*Introduction to the Koran*] (Paris: Maisonneuve et Larose, 1947); Jacques Berque, *Le Coran. Essai de traduction* [*The Koran: An Attempt at Translation*] (Paris: Albin Michel, 1995), 2nd edn; *Encyclopaedia of the Qur'ân*, under the direction of Jane Dammen McAuliffe et al., 5 vols., (Leiden: Brill, 2001–6); *The Blackwell Companion to the Qur'ân* (London: Blackwell, 2006); *Dictionnaire du Coran* [*Dictionary of the Koran*], under the direction of Mohammad Ali Amir-Moezzi (Paris: Robert Laffont, 2007); Mehdi Azaiez and Sabrina Melvin, *Le Coran, nouvelles approaches* [*The Koran: New Approaches*] (Paris: CNRS Éditions, 2013).

§42. – On the concepts of *sharia* and *fiqh*: Joseph Schacht, *An Introduction to Islamic Law* (Oxford: Clarendon Press, 1964); Louis Milliot and François-Paul Blanc, *Introduction à l'étude du droit musulman* [*Introduction to the Study of Islamic Law*] (Paris: Dalloz, 1987), 2nd edn; Abd al-Wahhâb Khallâf, *Les Fondements du droit musulman* [*The Foundations of Islamic Law*] (Paris: al-Qualam, 1997); Baber Johansen, *Contingency in a Sacred Law: Legal and Ethical Norms in the Muslim Fiqh* (Leiden: Brill, 1999); Hervé Bleuchot, *Droit musulman* [*Islamic Law*], vol. I, *Histoire* [*History*] (Aix-en-Provence: Presses universitaires d'Aix-Marseille, 2000); Dominique Urvoy, *Histoire de la pensée arabe et islamique* [*History of Arab and Islamic Thought*] (Paris: Seuil, 2006); Bernard G. Weiss, *The Spirit of Islamic Law* (Athens: University of Georgia Press, 2006); Jean-Paul Charnay, *Esprit du droit musulman* [*The Spirit of Islamic Law*] (Paris: Dalloz, 2008); Wael B. Hallaq, *Shari'a: Theory, Practice, Transformations* (Cambridge: Cambridge University Press 2009); Baudouin Dupret, *La Charia. Des sources à la pratique, un concept pluriel* [*Sharia: from the Sources to Practice, a Plural Concept*] (Paris: La Découverte, 2014). – On the formation of Islamic Right and its Methods: Joseph Schacht, *The Origins of Mahommadan Jurisprudence* (Oxford: Clarendon Press, 1950); Noel J. Coulson, *A History of Islamic Law* (Edinburgh: Edinburgh University Press, 1964); Henri De Wael, *Le Droit musulman. Nature et evolution* [*Islamic Law: Its Nature and*

Development] (CHEAM, 1993), 2nd edn; Norman Calder, *Studies in Early Muslim Jurisprudence* (Oxford: Clarendon Press, 1993); Harald Motzki, *The Origins of Islamic Jurisprudence: Meccan Fiqh before the Classical Schools*, trans. Marion Katz (Leiden: Brill, 2002); Wael J. Hallaq, *The Origins and Evolution of Islamic Law* (Cambridge: Cambridge University Press 2005).

§43. – On Shâfi'i: *al-Shâfi'i's Risala. Treatise on the Foundation of Islamic Jurisprudence*, trans. Majid Khadduri (Cambridge: Islamic Texts Society, 1961); Noel J. Coulson, *A History of Islamic Law*, *op. cit.*; Wael J. Hallaq, *A History of Islamic Legal Theories: An Introduction to Sunnî Usûl al-Fiqh* (Cambridge: Cambridge University Press 1997); Dominique Urvoy, *Histoire de la pensée arabe et islamique*, *op. cit.*

§44. – On the concept of *qiyâs*: Raymond Charles, *Le Droit musulman [Islamic Law]* (Paris: Puf, 1956); Joseph Schacht, *Introduction au droit musulman*, *op. cit.*; Louis Milliot and François-Paul Blanc, *Introduction à l'étude du droit musulman*, *op. cit.*; Hervé Bleuchot, *Droit musulman*, vol. I, *Histoire*, *op. cit.*; François-Paul Blanc, *Le droit musulman* (Paris: Dalloz, 2007).

§46. – On the distinction between *furû* and *usûl*: Louis Milliot and François-Paul Blanc, *Introduction à l'étude du droit musulman*, *op. cit.*; Wael B. Hallaq, *A History of Islamic Legal Theories*, *op. cit.*

§47. – On the concepts of *ijtihâd* and *taqlîd*: Joseph Schacht, *Introduction au droit musulman*, *op. cit.*; Wael J. Hallaq, 'Was the Gate of Ijtihad Closed?', *International Journal of Middle East Studies* 16/1n (1984), pp. 3–41; Hervé Bleuchot, *Droit musulman*, vol. I, *Histoire*, *op. cit.*; Wael J. Hallaq, *The Origins and Evolution of Islamic Law*, *op. cit.*

§48. – On extraordinary cases in Islamic Right: Ignaz Goldziher, *Le Dogme et la Loi dans l'islam* (1910), trans. fr. Félix Arin (Paris: L'Éclat, 2005).

§49. – On Ibn Khaldun and the *tasawwuf*: Arthur J. Arberry, *Sufism: An Account of the Mystics of Islam* (London: Allen & Unwin, 1950); Ibn Khaldun, *La Voie et la loi [The Path and the Law]*, trans. fr. René Pérez (Arles: Actes Sud, 1991); Sabrina Mervin, *Histoire de l'islam. Doctrines et fondements*, *op. cit.*

Interlude 5

§F. – On the concept of 'person': Yan Thomas, 'Le Sujet concret et la personne. Essai d'histoire juridique rétrospective' ['The Concrete Subject and the Person: An Essay in Retrospective Juridical History'], in Olivier Cayla and Yan Thomas, *Du droit de ne pas naître. À propos de l'affaire Perruche* [*On the Right not to be Born: Concerning the 'affaire Perruche'*] (Paris: Gallimard, 2002), pp. 89–170.

Chapter 6

§51. – On Confucius: Marcel Granet, *La Pensée chinoise* [*Chinese Thought*] (Paris: La Renaissance du Livre, 1934); Herrlee G. Creel, *Confucius: The Man and the Myth* (New York: John Day, 1949); Etiemble, *Confucius* (1966) (Paris: Gallimard, 1985), 2nd edn; Herbert Fingarette, *Confucius. The Secular as Sacred* (New York: Harper & Row, 1972); *Entretiens de Confucius* [*Analects*], trans. fr. Anne Cheng (Paris: Seuil, 1981); David L. Hall and Roger T. Ames, *Thinking Through Confucius* (Albany: State University of New York Press, 1987); Anne Cheng, *Histoire de la pensée chinoise* [*History of Chinese Thought*] (Paris: Seuil, 1997); Jean Levi, *Confucius* (Paris: Albin Michel, 2003); Ann-ping Chin, *The Authentic Confucius: A Life of Thought and Politics* (New York: Scribner, 2007). – On the historical context: Marcel Granet, *Chinese Civilization*, trans. Kathleen E. Innes and Mabel R. Brailsford (London: Kegan Paul, Trench, Trubner, 1930); René Grousset, *Histoire de la Chine. Des origines à la seconde guerre mondiale* [*History of China: From the Origins until the Second World War*] (Paris: Fayard, 1942); Jacques Gernet, *Le Monde chinois* [*The Chinese World*] (Paris: Armand Colin, 1972); John K. Fairbank and Mercle C. Goodman, *China: A New History* (Cambridge, MA: Harvard University Press, 2006), 2nd rev. edn; Quang Dang Vu, *Histoire de la Chine antique. Des origines à la fin des printemps et automne (546 av. J.-C.)* [*History of Ancient China: from the Origins until the End of the Spring and Autumn Period (546 BCE)*], 2 vols. (Paris: L'Harmattan, 2011). – On the concept of *li*: Jean Escarra, *Le Droit chinois. Conception et évolution.*

Institutions législatives et judiciaires. Science et enseignement [*Chinese Right: Conception and Development: Legislative and Judicial Institutions. Science and Teaching*] (Paris: Sirey, 1936); Joseph Needham, 'Human Law and the Law of Nature', in *Chinese Science* (London: Pilot Press, 1945); Derk Bodde, 'Basic Concepts of Chinese Law: The Genesis and Evolution of Legal Thought in Traditional China' (1963), *Essays on Chinese Civilization*, ed. Charles Le Blanc and Dorothy Borei (Princeton, NJ: Princeton University Press, 1981), pp. 171–194; Léon Vandermeersch, *Wangdao, ou la Voie royale. Recherches sur l'esprit des institutions de la Chine archaïque* [*Wangdao, or the Royal Way: Investigations Into the Spirit of Ancient Chinese Institutions*], 2 vols. (Paris: Publication de l'EFEO, 1977–80); Tsien Tche-hao, *Le Droit chinois* [*Chinese Right*] (Paris: PUF, 1982); Léon Vandermeersch, 'Droit et rites en Chine' ['Right and Rites in China'], in *Université de tous les savoirs*, vol. 8, *La Chine aujourd'hui* [*China Today*], under the direction of Yves Michaud (Paris: Odile Jacob, 2006), pp. 109–123; François Jullien, *L'Invention de l'idéal et le destin de l'Europe* [*The Invention of the Ideal and the Fate of Europe*] (Paris: Seuil, 2009); Olivier Beydon, *Introduction à la pensée juridique chinoise* [*Introduction to Chinese Juridical Thinking*] (Brussels: Larcier, 2015).

§52. – On the etymology of *li*: Jean Escarra, *Le Droit chinois, op. cit.*; Léon Vandermeersch, *Wangdao, ou la Voie royale, op. cit.*; Anne Cheng, *Histoire de la pensée chinoise, op. cit.*; Olivier Beydon, *Introduction à la pensée juridique chinoise, op. cit.* – On the institutionalization of rites under the Zhou: Herrlee G. Creel, *The Origins of Statecraft in China*, vol. 1, *The Western Chou Empire* (Chicago, IL: Chicago University Press, 1970); Quang Dang Vu, *Histoire de la Chine antique, op. cit.*

§53. – On the Chinese understanding of relations: Marcel Granet, *La Pensée chinoise, op. cit.*; Qu Tongzu, *Law and Society in Traditional China* (Paris: Mouton, 1961); Geoffrey MacCormack, *The Spirit of Traditional Chinese Law* (Athens: University of Georgia Press, 1996); Ivan P. Kamenarovic, *Le Conflit. Perceptions chinoise et occidentale* [*Conflict: Chinese and Western Perspectives*] (Paris: Cerf, 2001); François Jullien, *L'Invention de l'idéal et le destin de l'Europe, op. cit.*; Olivier Beydon, *Introduction à la pensée juridique chinoise, op. cit.*

§54. – On the concept of *ren*: Anne Cheng, *Histoire de la pensée chinoise, op. cit.*; Olivier Beydon, *Introduction à la pensée juridique chinoise, op. cit.*

§55. – On the concept of *xing*: Jean Escarra, *Le Droit chinois, op. cit.*; Derk Bodde, 'Basic Concepts of Chinese Law: The Genesis and Evolution of Legal Thought in Traditional China', *op. cit.*; Tsien Tche-hao, *Le Droit chinois, op. cit.*; François Jullien, *L'Invention de l'déal et le destin de l'Europe, op. cit.*; Jérôme Bourgon, 'Principe de légalité et règle de droit dans la tradition juridique chinoise' ['The Principle of Legality and the Rule of Law in the Chinese Juridical Tradition', in *La Chine et la démocratie* [*China and Democracy*], under the direction of Mireille Delmas-Marty and Pierre-Étienne Will (Paris: Fayard, 2007), pp. 157–174; Olivier Beydon, *Introduction à la pensée juridique chinoise, op. cit.*

§56. – On Legalism: Léon Vandermeersch, *La Formation du légisme. Recherche sur la constitution d'une philosophie politique caractéristique de la Chine ancienne* [*The Formation of Legalism: Investigations Into the Constitution of a Political Philosophy Distinctive of Ancient China*] (Paris: Publications de l'EFEO, 1965); Anne Cheng, *Histoire de la pensée chinoise, op. cit.*; Jean Levi, *Les Fonctionnaires divins. Politiques, despotisme et mystique en Chine ancienne* [*The Divine Officials: Politicians, Despotism and Belief in Ancient China*] (Paris: Seuil, 1989); Xu Zhen Zhou, *L'Art de la politique chez les légistes chinois* [*The Art of Politics in Chinese Legalism*] (Paris: Economica, 1995). – On the concept of *fa*: Jean Escarra, *Le Droit chinois, op. cit.*; Derk Bodde, 'Basic Concepts of Chinese Law: The Genesis and Evolution of Legal Thought in Traditional China', *op. cit.*; Tsien Tchehao, *Le Droit chinois, op. cit.*; Geoffrey MacCormack, *op. cit.*; Françoise Lauwaert, *Le Meurtre en famille. Parricide et infanticide en Chine (XVIIIe–XIXe siècle)* [*Murder in the Family: Parricide and Infanticide in China (18th–19th Century)*] (Paris: Odile Jacob, 1999); Romain Graziani, 'La complétude des amputés. Réflexions sur la loi, le rite et les parias en Chine ancienne' ['The Completeness of Amputees: Reflections on the Law, Rites and Pariahs in Ancient China'], in *Les Corps dans le taoïsme ancien. L'infirme, l'informe, l'infâme* [*Bodies in Ancient Taoism: The Infirm, the Deformed and the Repugnant*] (Paris: Les Belles Lettres, 2011); Olivier Beydon, *Introduction à la pensée juridique chinoise, op. cit.*

§57. – On Shang Yang: Léon Vandermeersch, *La Formation du légisme*, *op. cit.*; Li Yu-ning, *Shang Yang's Reforms and State Control in China* (London: Routledge, 1977); Anne Cheng, *Histoire de la pensée chinoise*, *op. cit.*; *Le livre du prince Shang* [*The Book of Lord Shang*], trans. fr. Jean Levi (Paris: Flammarion, 2005).

§58. – On Maître Xun: Anne Cheng, *Histoire de la pensée chinoise*, *op. cit.*; *Écrits de maître Xun* [*The Writings of Xun Kuang*], trans. fr. Ivan P. Kamenarovic (Paris: Les Belles Lettres, 2016).

§59. – On the development of the Confucian understanding of Right: Jean Escarra, *Le Droit chinois*, *op. cit.*; Tsien Tche-hao, *Le Droit chinois*, *op. cit.*; Anne Cheng, *Histoire de la pensée chinoise*, *op. cit.*; Olivier Beydon, *Introduction à la pensée juridique chinoise*, *op. cit.*

§60. – On judicial procedure in ancient China: *Affaires résolues à l'ombre du poirier. Un manuel chinois de jurisprudence et d'investigation policière du XIIIe siècle* [*Cases Decided in the Shade of a Pear Tree: A Chinese Manual of Jurisprudence and Police Investigation from the 13th Century*], ed. Robert Van Gulik (1956), trans. fr. Lisa Bresner and Jacques Limoni (Paris: Albin Michel, 2002).

Interlude 6

§G. – On the sanction: Laurent de Sutter, *Poétique de la police* [*Poetics of Policing*] (Aix-en-Provence: Rouge Profond, 2017).

Chapter 7

§61. – On *ritsuryô* and Prince Shôtoku's reforms: André Gonthier, *Histoire des institutions japonaises* [*History of Japanese Institutions*] (Brussels: Éditions de la librairie encyclo-pédique, 1956); Yosiyuki Noda, *Introduction au droit japonais* [*Introduction to Japanese Right*] (Paris: Dalloz, 1966); Mitsusada Inoue, 'The Ritsuryô System in Japan', *Acta Asiatica* 31 (1977), pp. 83–112; Jean-Hubert Moitry, *Le Droit japonais* [*Japanese Right*] (Paris: PUF, 1988); Carl Steenstrup, *A History of Law in Japan until 1868* (Leiden: Brill, 1996), 2nd edn. – On the historical context: Edwin O. Reischauer, *Histoire du Japon et des Japonais* [*History of Japan and the Japanese*], trans. fr. Richard Dubreuil (Paris: Seuil, 1973); *L'Histoire du Japon, des origines à nos jours* [*History of Japan, from the Origins to the Present Day*] under the direction of Francine Hérail (Paris: Hermann, 2010); Pierre-François Souyri, *Nouvelle histoire du Japon* [*New History of Japan*] (Paris: Perrin, 2010).

§62. – On the Tang Code: Jean Escarra, *Le Droit chinois*, *op. cit.*; *The Great Tang Code*, vol. 1, *General Principles*, trans. Johnson Wallace (Princeton, NJ: Princeton University Press, 1979); Tsien Tche-hao, *Le Droit chinois*, *op. cit.*; Olivier Beydon, *Introduction à la pensée juridique chinoise*, *op. cit.* – On the reception of the Tang Code in Japan: Carl Steenstrup, *A History of Law in Japan until 1868*, *op. cit.*; Francine Hérail, *L'Histoire du Japon, des origines à nos jours*, *op. cit.*

§63. – On the 'seventeen articles': Katsumi Kuroita, 'Prince Shôtoku and His Seventeen-Articles Constitution', *Cultural Nippon* 8 (1940), pp. 49–74; *Sources of Japanese Tradition*, vol. 1, *From Earliest Time to 1600* (1958), under the direction of W. Theodore de Bary et al. (New York: Columbia University Press 2010), 2nd edn; Carl Steenstrup, *A History of Law in Japan until 1868*, *op. cit.*

§64. – On the concept of *horitsu*: Yosiyuki Noda, *Introduction au droit japonais*, *op. cit.*; Dominique T. C. Wang, *Les Sources du droit japonais* [*The Sources of Japanese Right*] (Geneva: Droz, 1978).

§65. – On the concepts of *giri* and *ninjō*: Yosiyuki Noda, *Introduction au droit japonais*, *op. cit.*; Jean-Hubert Moitry, *Le Droit japonais*, *op. cit.*; Hiroshi Oda, *Japanese Law* (1992) (Oxford: Oxford University Press, 2011), 3rd edn.

§66. – On the emotional aspect of Japanese Right: Yosiyuki Noda, *Introduction au droit japonais*, *op. cit.*

§67. – On the concept of *on*: Ruth Benedict, *The Chrysanthemum and the Sword: Patterns of Japanese Culture* (London: Secker & Warburg, 1947).

§69. – On the *kyaku*: *Recueil de décrets des trois ères méthodiquement classés* [*Collection of Decrees from Three*

Eras Methodically Classed], trans. fr. Francine Hérail, 2 vols., (Geneva: Droz, 2008–11).

§70. – On the victory of juridical Confucianism under the Tokugawa dynasty: Masao Maruyama, *Essais sur l'histoire de la pensée politique au Japon* [*Essays on the History of Political Thought in Japan*] (1952), trans. fr. Jacques Joly (Paris: PUF, 1996); Yosiyuki Noda, *Introduction au droit japonais, op. cit.*; Carl Steenstrup, *A History of Law in Japan until 1868, op. cit.* – On the refusal of Right in Japan: Jean-Hubert Moitry, *Le Droit japonais, op. cit.*; John Owen Haley, *The Spirit of Japanese Law* (Athens: University of Georgia Press, 1998).

Interlude 7

§H. – On reason: Pierre Schlag, *The Enchantement of Reason* (Durham, NC: Duke University Press, 1998).

Chapter 8

§71. – On the concept of *smriti*: Louis Renou, *La Civilisation de l'Inde ancienne, d'après les textes sanskrits* [*Ancient Indian Civilization, Based on Sanskrit Texts*] (Paris: Flammarion, 1950). – On the concept of *dharma*: Robert Lingat, *Les Sources du droit dans le système traditionnel de l'Inde* [*Sources of Right in the Traditional System of India*] (Paris: Mouton, 1967); Madeleine Biardeau, *L'Hindousime. Anthropologie d'une civilisation* [*Hinduism: Anthropology of a Civilization*] (1972) (Paris: Flammarion, 1981), 2nd edn; Albrecht Wezler, 'Dharma in the Vedas and the Dharmasâstras', *Journal of Indian Philosophy* 32 (2004), pp. 629–654; *Dharma. Studies in its Semantic, Cultural and Religious History*, under the direction of Patrick Olivelle (Delhi: Motilal Banarsidass, 2009); Donald R. Davis, Jr., *The Spirit of Hindu Law* (Cambridge: Cambridge University Press, 2010); Bina Gupta, *An Introduction to Indian Philosophy. Perspectives on Reality, Knowledge and Freedom* (London: Routledge, 2012); *A Dharma Reader. Classical Indian Law*, ed. Patrick Olivelle (New York: Columbia University Press 2016).

§72. – On the *Dharmasutra*: Sures Chandra Banerji,

Dharma-sûtras. A Study in their Origin and Development (Calcutta: Punthi Pustak, 1962); Pandurang Vaman Kane, *History of Dharmaśâstra*, 5 vols. (Poona: BORI, 1962–75); Louis Renou, 'Sur le genre du *sûtra* dans la littérature sanskrite' ['On the *Sutra* Genre in Sanskrit Literature'], *Journal asiatique* 251 (1963), pp. 165–216 ; Robert Lingat, *Les Sources du droit dans le système traditionnel de l'Inde*, op. cit.; *Studies in Dharmaśâstra*, under the direction of Richard Lariviere (Calcutta: Firma KLM, 1984); *Dharmasutras. The Law Code of Ancient India*, trans. Patrick Olivelle (Oxford: Oxford University Press, 1999); Donald R. Davis, Jr., *The Spirit of Hindu Law*, op. cit.; Ludo Rocher, *Studies in Hindu Law and Dharmaśâstra*, ed. Donald R. Davis, Jr. (London: Anthem, 2014). – On the *varna*: Louis Renou, *La Civilisation de l'Inde ancienne*, op. cit.; Louis Dumont, *Homo hierarchicus. Le système des castes et ses implications* [*Homo Hierarchicus: The Caste System and Its Implications*] (Paris: Gallimard, 1966); Robert Lingat, *Les Sources du droit dans le système traditionnel de l'Inde*, op. cit. – On sacrifice in India: Madeleine Biardeau and Charles Malamoud, *Le Sacrifice dans l'Inde ancienne* [*Sacrifice in Ancient India*] (Paris: PUF, 1976); Charles Malamoud, *La Danse des pierres. Étude sur la scène sacrificielle dans l'Inde ancienne* [*The Dance of Stones: A Study of the Sacrificial Scene in Ancient India*] (Paris: Seuil, 2005).

§73. – On the *trivarga*: Madeleine Biardeau, *L'Hindouisme. Anthropologie d'une civilisation*, op. cit.; Bina Gupta, *An Introduction to Indian Philosophy*, op. cit.

§74. – On *pramana*: Donald R. Davis, Jr., *The Spirit of Hindu Law*, op. cit.

§75. – On the concept of *danda*: *ibid.*

§77. – On *Kautilya*: Roger Boesche, *The First Great Political Realist. Kautilya and His Arthashastra* (Lanham, MD: Lexington, 2002); Patrick Olivelle, *King, Governance and Law in Ancient India. Kautilya's Arthashastra* (Oxford: Oxford University Press, 2013).

§79. – On the Laws of Manu: Robert Lingat, *Les Sources du droit dans le système traditionnel de l'Inde*, op. cit.; Heramba Chatterjee, *The Law of Debt in Ancient India* (Calcutta: Sanskrit College, 1971); Nikunja Vihari Banerjee, *Studies in the Dharmaśâstra of Manu* (New Delhi: Munshiram Manoharlal,

1980); *The Law Code of Manu*, trans. Patrick Olivelle (Oxford: Oxford University Press, 2004).

§80. – On Emperor Asoka: Romila Thapar, *Ashoka and the Decline of the Mauryas* (Oxford: Oxford University Press, 1973); *Les Inscriptions d'Asoka* [*The Inscriptions of Asoka*], trans. fr. Jules Bloch (Paris: Les Belles Lettres, 2007); Charles Allen, *Ashoka. The Search for India's Lost Emperor* (London: Hachette, 2012); *Reimagining Asoka. Memory and History*, under the direction of Patrick Olivelle et al. (Oxford: Oxford University Press, 2012); Michel Angot, *Histoire des Indes* [*History of the Indies*] (Paris: Les Belles Lettres, 2017).

Interlude 8

§I. – On judgement: Gilles Deleuze, 'Pour en finir avec le jugement' ['Finishing with Judgement'], *Critique et clinique* [*Criticism and Clinic*] (Paris: Minuit, 1993), pp. 158–169. See also Laurent de Sutter, *Deleuze, la pratique du droit* [*Deleuze, the Practice of Right*] (Paris: Michalon, 2009).

Chapter 9

§81. – On the origins of government in ancient Egypt: Nicolas Grimal, *Histoire de l'Égypte ancienne* [*History of Ancient Egypt*] (Paris: Fayard, 1988); Jean Vercoutter, *L'Égypte et la vallée du Nil* [*Egypt and the Nile Valley*], vol. 1, *Des origines à la fin de l'Ancien Empire. 12000–2000 av. J.-C.* [*From the Origins until the End of the Ancient Empire: 12000–2000 BCE*] (Paris: PUF, 1992); Dominique Valbelle, *Histoire de l'État pharaonique* [*History of the Pharaonic State*] (Paris: PUF, 1998); Beatrix Midant-Reynes, *The Prehistory of Egypt. From the First Egyptians to the First Pharaohs* (London: Blackwell, 2000); Damien Agut and Juan-Carlos Moreno Garcia, *L'Égypte des pharaons. De Narmer à Dioclétien. 3150 av. J.-C.-284 apr. J.-C.* [*Egypt of the Pharaohs: From Narmer to Diocletian, 3150 BCE–284 CE*] (Paris: Belin, 2016).

§82. – On *maât*: Jan Assmann, *Maât. L'Égypte pharaonique et l'dée de justice sociale* [*Maât: Pharaonic Egypt and the Idea of Social Justice*] (Paris: Julliard, 1989); Miriam Lichtheim, *Maât in Egyptian Autobiographies and Related Studies* (Göttingen: Vandenhoeck & Ruprecht, 1992); Aristide Théodoridès, *Vivre de Maât. Travaux sur le droit égyptien ancien* [*Living by Maât: Works on Egyptian Right*], ed. Jean-Marie Kruchten, 2 vols. (Brussels: Société belge d'études orientales, 1995); Emily Teeter, *The Presentation of Maât. Ritual and Legitimacy in Ancient Egypt* (Chicago, IL: The Oriental Institute, 1997); Bernadette Menu, *Maât. L'ordre juste du monde* [*Maât: The Just Order of the World*] (Paris: Michalon, 2005); Bernadette Menu, 'Maât, l'ordre social et inégalités dans l'Égypte ancienne. De l'apport égyptien au concept gréco-romain de justice' ['Maât, Social Order and Inequalities in Ancient Egypt: From the Egyptian Contribution to the Greco-Roman concept of Justice'], *Droit et cultures* 69/1 (2015), pp. 51–73.

§83. – On the concept of *isfet*: Jan Assmann, *Maât. L'Égypte pharaonique et l'idée de justice sociale, op. cit.*; Bernadette Menu, *Maât, op. cit.*

§84. – On the moral of *The Eloquent Peasant*: Gustave Lefebvre, *Romans et contes égyptiens de l'époque pharaonique* [*Egyptian Romances and Tales in the Pharaonic Era*] (Paris: Maisonneuve, 1949); Jan Assmann, *Maât. L'Égypte pharaonique et l'idée de justice sociale, op. cit.*

§86. – On the literary genre of tomb inscriptions: Jan Assmann, *Maât. L'Égypte pharaonique et l'idée de justice sociale, op. cit.* – On the juridical dimension of the Book of the Dead: Paul Barguet, *Le Livre des morts des anciens Égyptiens* [*The Ancient Egyptians' Book of the Dead*] (Paris: Cerf, 1967); Bernadette Menu, *Maât, op. cit.*

§87. – On the concept of *ba*: Louis V. Zabkar, *A Study of the Ba Concept in Ancient Egyptian Texts* (Chicago, IL: University of Chicago Press, 1968); Jan Assmann, *Maât. L'Égypte pharaonique et l'idée de justice sociale, op. cit.*

§88. – On the activity of judging in ancient Egypt: Bernadette Menu, 'Aspects de la fonction de juger dans l'Égypte pharaonique' ['Aspects of the Function of Judging in Pharaonic Egypt'], *La Fonction de juger. Égypte ancienne et Mésopotamie* [*The Function of Judging: Ancient Egypt and Mesopotamia*], under the direction of Bernadette Menu, *Droit et cultures* 47/1 (2004), pp. 123–138; Bernadette Menu, *Maât, op. cit.*

§89. – On *hépou*: Aristide Théodoridès, 'À propos de la loi dans l'Égypte ancienne' ['Regarding Law in Ancient Egypt'] (1967), *Vivre de Maât, op. cit*, pp. 21–68; *Le Droit égyptien ancien* [*Right in Ancient Egypt*], under the direction of Aristide Théodoridès (Brussels: Institut des hautes études de Belgique, 1976); Bernadette Menu, *Maât, op. cit*.

§90. – On the idea of *nefer*: Jan Assman, *Maât. L'Égypte pharaonique et l'idée de justice sociale, op. cit*.

Interlude 9

§J. – On politics and policing : Jacques Rancière, *La Mésentente. Politique et philosophie* [*Bad Blood: Politics and Philosophy*] (Paris: Galilée, 1995).

Chapter 10

§91. – On the Torah and the Talmud: Menachem Elom, *Jewish Law. History, Sources, Principles* (1973), trans. Bernard Auerbach and Melvyn J. Skyes, 4 vols. (Philadelphia: Jewish Publication Society, 1994); 'Talmud', *Dictionnaire encyclopédique du judaïsme* [*Encyclopedic Dictionary of Judaism*], under the direction of Geoffrey Wigoder, trans. fr. under the direction of Sylvie Anne Goldberg (Paris: Cerf/Robert Laffont, 1996), pp. 982–987; 'Torah', *ibid.*, pp. 1013–1016; Adin Steinsaltz, *Introduction au Talmud* [*Introduction to the Talmud*] (Paris: Albin Michel, 2002); Rémi Brague, 'Torah', *Vocabulaire européen des philosophes, op. cit.*, pp. 1296–1298; Nathan E. Lopes Cardozo, *The Written and Oral Torah. A Comprehensive Introduction* (Lanham, MD: Jason Aronson, 2004); Julien Darmon, 'Torah écrite et Torah orale. L'architecture du savoir talmudique' ['Written Torah and Oral Torah: The Architecture of Talmudic Knowledge'], in *Les Lieux de savoir* [*Places of Knowledge*], vol. 2, *Les Mains de l'intellect* [*The Hands of the Intellect*], under the direction of Christian Jacob (Paris: Albin Michel, 2011), pp. 724–743; Patrice Bloch and Yossef Berdah, *Les Secrets de la Torah orale. La méthodologie rabbinique au fil des siècles* [*The Secrets of the Oral Torah: The Rabbinic Method through the Centuries*] (Paris: PUF, 2012). – On the historical context: André Chouraqui, *Histoire du judaïsme* [*History of Judaism*] (Paris: PUF, 1957); Étienne Nodet, *Essai sur les origines du judaïsme. De Josué aux pharisiens* [*Essay on the Origins of Judaism: from Joshua to the Pharisees*] (Paris: Cerf, 1992); *Aux origines du judaïsme* [*To the Origins of Judaism*], under the direction of Jean Baumgarten and Julien Darmon (Arles/Paris: Actes Sud/Les Liens qui libèrent, 2012); Simon Claude Mimouni, *Le Judaïsme ancien du VIe siècle avant notre ère au IIIe siècle de notre ère. Des prêtres aux rabbins* [*Ancient Judaism from the 6th Century* BCE *to the 3rd Century* CE: *From Priests to Rabbis*] (Paris: PUF, 2012); Michel Abitbol, *Histoire des Juifs. De la Genèse à nos jours* [*History of Jews: From Genesis to the Present*] (Paris: Perrin, 2013).

§92. – On the Halakha and the Aggadah: Isaac Heineman, *La Loi dans la pensée juive* [*Law in Jewish Thought*], trans. fr. Charles Touati (Paris: Albin Michel, 1962); Menachem Elom, *Jewish Law*, vol. 2, *The Legal Sources of Jewish Law*, op. cit.; Ephraïm E. Urbach, *The Halakhah. Its Sources and Development* (S.l.: Yad la-Talmud, 1986); Joel Roth, *The Halakhic Process. A Systematic Analysis* (Jerusalem: JTS Press, 1986); 'Aggadah', *Dictionnaire ecyclopédique du judaïsme*, op. cit., pp. 26–27; 'Halakha', *ibid.*, pp. 412–419; François-Xavier Licari, *Le Droit talmudique* [*Talmudic Right*] (Paris: Dalloz, 2015).

§93. – On justification: François-Xavier Licari, *Le Droit talmudique*, op. cit. – On rabbinic methods of interpretation: Menachem Elom, *Jewish Law*, op. cit.; Joel Roth, *The Halakhic Process. A Systematic Analysis*, op. cit.; Gabriel Abitbol, *Logique du droit talmudique* [*The Logic of Talmudic Right*] (Paris: Éditions des sciences hébraïques, 1993); Dan Jaffé, *Essai sur l'interprétation et la culture talmudiques. Femmes et familles dans le Talmud* [*Essay on Talmudic Culture and Interpretation: Women and Families in the Talmud*] (Paris, Cerf, 2013).

§94. – On Maimonides: Moïse Maïmonide, *Le Guide des égarés, suivi du Traité des huit chapitres* [*Guide for the Perplexed, followed by The Eight Chapters*], trans. fr. Salomon Munk (Lagrasse: Verdier, 1979); Léo Strauss, *Maïmonide*, trans. fr. (Paris: PUF, 2012); Maurice-Ruben Hayoun, *Maïmonide, ou l'autre Moïse : 1138–1204* [*Maimonides, or the Other Moses: 1138–1204*] (Paris: Jean-Claude Lattès, 1994); Gérard Haddad, *Maïmonide* (Paris: Les Belles Lettres, 1998); Pierre Bouretz,

Lumières du Moyen Âge. Maïmonide philosophe [*Lights of the
Middle Ages: Maimonides the Philosopher*] (Paris: Gallimard,
2015).

§95. – On the distinction between 'monetary' and the 'forbidden
and permitted': François-Xavier Licari, *Le Droit talmudique, op.
cit.* – On Chaim of Volozhin: Rabbi Haïm de Volozine, *L'Âme
de la vie* [*The Soul of Life*], trans. fr. Benjamin Gross (Lagrasse:
Verdier, 1986).

§96. – On the principle *lifnim mi-shurat ha-din*: François-Xavier
Licari, *Le Droit talmudique, op. cit.*

§97. – On halakhic pluralism: *Ibid.*

§98. – On the concept of *mishpatim*: *Ibid.* – On the rule for
granting exceptions in Talmudic Right: Georges Hansel, 'La Loi
du royaume est la loi' ['The Law of the Kingdom is the Law'],
Explorations talmudiques [*Talmudic Explorations*] (Paris: Odile
Jacob, 1998), p. 143–152; Yaacov Feit, 'The Prohibition against
Going to Secular Courts', *The Journal of the Beth Din of
America* 1 (2012), p. 30–47.

§99. – On 'Jacob's Well': *Aggadoth du Talmud de Babylone. La
source de Jacob* [*Aggadoth of the Babylonian Talmud: Jacob's
Source*], trans. fr. Arlette Elkaïm-Sartre (Lagrasse: Verdier, 1982).
– On Bialik: *Hayyim Nahman Bialik, Halakha et Aggada*, trans.
fr. Jean Getzel (Paris: L'Éclat, 2017).

Index